Semantics, Stylistics and Pedagogics

Semantics, Stylistics and Pedagogics

V. Prakasam and Anvita Abbi

Allied Publishers Pvt. Ltd.
NEW DELHI • MUMBAI • KOLKATA • CHENNAI • NAGPUR
AHMEDABAD • BANGALORE • HYDERABAD • LUCKNOW

Allied Publishers Private Limited

Regd. Off.: 1/13-14 Asaf Ali Road, New Delhi–110002
Ph.: 011-23239001 • E-mail: delhi.books@alliedpublishers.com

87/4, Chander Nagar, Alambagh, Lucknow–226005
Ph.: 0522-4012850 • E-mail: appltdlko9@gmail.com

17 Chittaranjan Avenue, Kolkata–700072
Ph.: 033-22129618 • E-mail: cal.books@alliedpublishers.com

15 J.N. Heredia Marg, Ballard Estate, Mumbai–400001
Ph.: 022-42126969 • E-mail: mumbai.books@alliedpublishers.com

60 Shiv Sunder Apartments (Ground Floor), Central Bazar Road,
Bajaj Nagar, Nagpur–440010
Ph.: 0712-2234210 • E-mail: ngp.books@alliedpublishers.com

F-1 Sun House (First Floor), C.G. Road, Navrangpura,
Ellisbridge P.O., Ahmedabad–380006
Ph.: 079-26465916 • E-mail: ahmbd.books@alliedpublishers.com

No. 25/10, Commander-in-chief Road, Ethiraj Lane (Next to Post Office)
Egmore, Chennai–600008
Ph.: 044-28523938 • E-mail: chennai.books@alliedpublishers.com

The Hebbar Sreevaishnava Sabha, Sudarshan Complex - 2
No. 22, Seshadri Road, Bangalore–560009
Ph.: 080-22262081 • E-Mail: bngl.books@alliedpublishers.com

3-2-844/6 & 7 Kachiguda Station Road, Hyderabad–500027
Ph.: 040-24619079 • E-mail: hyd.books@alliedpublishers.com

Website: www.alliedpublishers.com

© 2018, ALLIED PUBLISHERS PVT. LIMITED

No part of the material protected by this Copyright notice may be reproduced or utilized in any form or by any means, electronic or mechanical including photocopying, recording or by any information storage and retrieval system, without prior written permission from the copyright owners.

ISBN: 978-93-87380-45-5

Published by Sunil Sachdev and printed by Ravi Sachdev at
Allied Publishers Pvt. Ltd., (Printing Division), A-104 Mayapuri Phase II,
New Delhi-110064.

To

Professor Braj B. Kachru

Preface

Language is semogenic system, *i.e.*, meaning-creating system. Since there can be no meaning without expression, a language event is treated as "doubly articulated" system comprising a "plane of content" and the "expression plane". Meaning then is "the transduction of the phenomenal back into the phenomenal *via* these two interfaces of content and expression" (Halliday 2002 : 304-355) Halliday adds: "… meaning is a mode of action engaged at the intersection of the material (or phenomenal) and the conscious, as complementary modes of experience…. By the act of meaning, consciousness imposes order on the phenomena of experience" (ibid: 364).

Language, as a system though complex, is learnable and teachable. This has been made possible by the linguists who have shown it as describable.

Meaning, being the core of the existential reality of language, needs to be comprehended and analyzed, properly grasped and talked about. The first part of this book, 'Semantics', is planned to strengthen our comprehension of the "meaning" facet of language at 'isolable' level (lexical) and also at 'combinatorial' level (discoursal). The way 'meaning' is viewed and analyzed at different times and in different intellecting traditions is presented in the first three chapters which constitute the part called Semantics. The fourth chapter constitutes the second part of the book, 'Stylistics', dealing with the way 'meaning' is juiced out from a text. One can even say that we actually juice out meaning for a text because the meaning is actually a response from the aesthetic and cognitive capabilities of a reader. So the 'grasping' of meaning of a text is again a dynamic process comprising denotative, connotative and suggestive responses. The third part of the book is 'Pedagogics' which subsumes 'androgogics' too. Here we see how the language teacher who has comprehended and grasped 'meaning' conveys it to the student in the classroom. This conveying is actually facilitating comprehension and grasping in the minds of the students.

This tridental activity of 'meaning' study is expected to be of a great help to students, teachers and scholars working on different texts.

In his Foreword to an earlier version of a part of this book, Professor Braj B. Kachru very graciously said that the book was going to be useful to teachers, students and also teacher trainers and researchers.

This volume is intended to be richer and more comprehensive.

We also dedicate this book to the memory of Professor Braj B. Kachru with great admiration for his work and deep appreciation for his support to younger scholars.

V. Prakasam
Anvita Abbi

Contents

Preface		vii
Chapter I: The Tradition		1-18
1.1.	Introduction	1
1.1.0	Ancient Tradition: The Sphota Theory	3
1.1.1	The Apoha Theory	6
1.1.2	Modern Reflections of the Apoha Theory	7
1.1.3	The Linguistic Event	8
1.1.4	The Sentence	9
1.1.5	The Tātparya	10
1.1.6	Uddeśya and Vidheya	10
1.1.7	The Meaning of Words	11
1.1.8	Learning Word Meanings	11
1.1.9	Synonyms, Homonymy and Contextual Categories	12
1.1.10	Classification of Contextual Categories	14
1.1.11	Word and Sentence	14
1.1.12	The Primary Meaning of a Word	15
1.2.0	Pre-modern European Tradition: The Modistae	15
1.2.1	Port Royal Theory	17
Chapter II: The Recent Trends		19-76
2.1.0	Various Approaches to Recent Trends	19
2.1.1	Katz–Fodor Approach	19
2.1.2	Conceptual Relations	20
2.1.3	Katz's Views of a Semantic Theory	21
2.2.1	Weinreich's Model: The Lexical Entry	23
2.2.2	Linking	24
2.2.3	Transfer Feature	25
2.3.0	Generative Semantics: Lakoff, McCawley *et. al.*	25
2.3.1	Salient Features of Generative Semantics	26
2.3.2	Category Distinctions	29
2.3.3	Differences and Identity of Meaning	30

2.3.4	Universal Semantic Elements	33
2.3.5	Recent Developments in Generative Semantics	35
2.4.0	Generative Semantics: Chafe	38
2.4.1	Aspects of Chafe's Theory	39
2.4.2	Noun-Verb Relations	43
2.4.3	The Semantic Structure of a Sentence	47
2.4.4	Discussion Initiated by Chafe (1974, 1976)	49
2.5.0	Fillmore's Case Grammar (1968)	50
2.5.1	Communication and Presupposition	56
2.6.0	Chomsky's Views (1957)	57
2.6.1	Syntactic Structures (1957), Aspects (1965) and EST (1971)	57
2.6.2	Revised Extended Standard Theory (1975), Trace Theory, Government and Binding (1981)	59
2.7.0	Shaumyan's Theory	64
2.7.1	Genotype and Phenotype Grammars	65
2.7.2	Preference Semantics	67
2.8.0	Pragmatics	69
2.8.1	Performatives, Presuppositions and Conversational Postulates	69
2.8.2	Proposition	72
2.8.3	Opacity	72
2.8.4	Negation	74
2.8.5	Implicatures	75

Chapter III: The Contextual and Functional View of Meanings 77-97

3.1.0	Firth and Malinowski	77
3.1.1	Meaning and Contextual Relations	77
3.1.2	Levels of Meaning	79
3.2.1	Significance	83
3.2.2	Value	85
3.3.1	Lexis	87
3.3.2	Potentiality and Instantiality	90

Contents   xi

3.3.3	Summary	91
3.4.1	Hallidayan Functionalist Approach	91
3.4.2	Sememes and Pragmemes	94
3.4.3	Presupposition, Entailment and Implication	96
Chapter IV: Stylistics: Literary Semantics		**98-141**
4.1.0	Indian Poetics: An Overview	98
4.1.1	Bhāmaha	98
4.1.2	Rasa Theory	99
4.1.3	Dhvani Theory	99
4.1.4	Rīti	100
4.1.5	Auchitya	101
4.1.6	Vakrokti	102
4.1.7	Svabhāvokti	104
4.1.8	Sahṛdaya	105
4.2.0	Functional Stylistics	106
4.2.1	Prominence	106
4.2.2	Markedness	107
4.2.3	Cohesion	110
4.2.4	Clustering, Collocation and Colligation	111
4.2.5	Unity and Coupling	112
4.2.6	Rhythm	113
4.3.0	Metre and Rhythm	115
4.3.1	Metre Rhythm	117
4.3.2	Syllable and Foot	118
4.3.3	Verse Line	119
4.3.4	Synaloepha and Silent Ictus	120
4.4	Geralld Gould's 'Wander–Thirst'	120
4.5	Experiential Component	121
4.6	Interactional Component	123
4.7	Summative Words	124
4.8	Textual Component	124
4.9	Cohesion, Prominence and Unity	130
4.10	Metrical Pattern of the Poem	134
4.11	Semantic Rhythm	141

Chapter V: Pedagogics: Meaning and the Language Teacher 142-160

5.1.0	Levels of Meaning	142
5.1.1	Phonological Meaning	142
5.1.2	Grammar and Lexis	145
5.1.3	Collocation and Colligation	146
5.1.4	Content	148
5.2.0	Conclusions for the Teacher	149
5.2.1	The Teaching of Meaning	151
5.2.2	Problems of Meaning	154
5.3.1	Abstraction, Figures of Speech and Cultural Milieu	157
5.3.2	Summary	159

Glossary 161

Bibliography 191

Index 203

CHAPTER I
The Tradition

1.1 Introduction

What's 'meaning'? This is a problem which has been engaging the attention of philosophers, logicians and linguists for ages. Hence the voluminous research done on meaning, on 'meaning of meaning', on 'capturing meaning' and on 'conveying meaning'. In this monograph an attempt is made to (i) present a comprehensive view of meaning from the viewpoint of linguists (semantics), (ii) present a functional view of meaning of literary texts (stylistics) and (iii) state how best meaning can be conveyed in a language teaching situation (pedagogics).

Human life encompasses three worlds of experience: the cognitive, the physical and the linguistic. Corresponding to the three worlds we have three names which would constitute a triangle: *idea, item* and *label*. The cognitive idea is *represented* by the linguistic label and the linguistic label *signifies* the physical item. Here we include both concrete and abstract experience in the word 'physical'. The item *expounds* or *realizes* the idea. This relationship may be represented diagrammatically as shown in Figure 1. This triangle represents the ILI relationship:

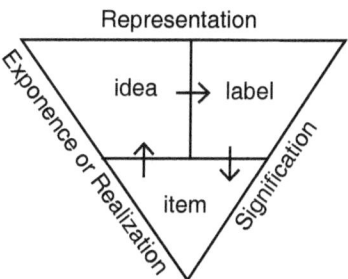

Fig. 1: ILI Triangular Box

This relationship can be represented in a different way as shown in Figure 2.

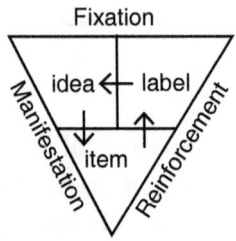

Fig. 2: ILI Triangular Box

In other words the idea is *manifested* in the item which expounds it; the idea is *fixed* in our minds by the label which represents it; the use of the label is *reinforced* by the item which is signified by the label. These are mutually defining relationships among the three different but complementary worlds of our experience (cf. Ziff, 1960 and Lee, 1941).

The ILI triangle can be fruitfully used in the communicative situation where side A represents the speaker and side B represents the hearer. Figure 3 gives the total picture of communication of meaning in the world of human experience.

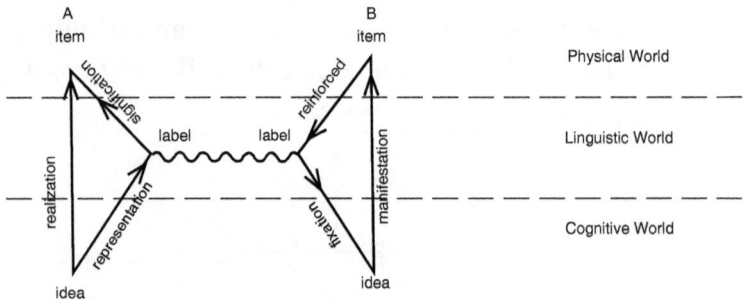

Fig. 3: The Communication of Meaning

'Meaning', as it is commonly understood, is a term used to capture the relationships mentioned above. This does not mean that all the "meaning-explorers" use the term with the same signification. The psychologist, the philosopher, the logician, the sociologist, the anthropologist and the linguist have each viewed 'meaning' from a specific angle. Here we shall investigate the problem of meaning from the linguist's point of view.

The linguist has many things to deal with while describing a given language: *sounds, forms* (structures and lexical items) and *meaning* conveyed by the linguistic patterns in a given situation. His view is contingent upon his purpose and his tools. We can see a long tradition of the study of meaning both in India and in Europe, especially Greece.

1.1.0 Ancient Tradition: The Sphota Theory

In Greek tradition, as is evident from Plato's *Republic,* there had been quite a long controversy between 'analogists' and 'anomalists'. The former school believed that there was a logical, or, say, 'etymological' relationship between meaning and the words of their language. The latter school did not agree with them and rather believed that it was more an irregular and arbitrary relationship that the words and their meanings had.

The ancient Indian tradition was more developed. We can have a good account of these Indian theories of meaning in Brough (1951, 1953), Kunjunni Raja (1963) and Pandeya (1963).

In the Indian (Sanskrit) tradition we find two main approaches to the study of meaning: the ***Khaṇḍapakṣha*** and the ***Akhaṇḍapakṣha***. The khaṇḍapakṣha approach believed in an analytical method. Here 'word' is the autonomous unit of thought and sense and the sentence is taken to be the concatenation of words. Grammarians like Pāṇini, Kātyayāna, Patañjali and Yāska took word as 'the point of origin' for their linguistic and semantic study. The akhaṇḍapakṣha school took sentence as the linguistic prime. This theory, advocated by Bhartṛhari, treated sentence as "a single integral symbol" and maintained that its meaning was conveyed by *sphoṭa*. This brings us to an important theory of meaning, viz., the sphoṭa theory. In formulating this theory Bhartṛhari followed in the footsteps of Auḍumbarāyaṇa and Vartākṣa.

Bhartṛhari looks at an utterance from two angles: (i) its sound pattern, and (ii) its meaning-bearing potentiality—the former being the external aspect and the latter the internal aspect. The internal aspect, which is directly associated with the meaning is sphoṭa, the partless integral linguistic symbol.

Patañjali considers sphoṭa as the permanent element in the word which may even be considered the essential word and distinguishes it from **dhvani** which is the actualized and ephemeral element and an attribute of the first. To Patañjali sphoṭa is not a single indivisible symbol considered as the meaning-bearer, as Bhartṛhari put it, but only the unchanging sound-unit or a time-series pattern of such units.

Each sound in an utterance helps in manifesting this sphoṭa, the first one vaguely, the next one more clearly, and so on, until the last one, aided by the impressions of the preceding perceptions reveals it clearly and distinctly. But it is important to remember that the sounds uttered to reveal this sphoṭa cannot be considered as parts of the essential word or sphoṭa but only as diacritical marks to reveal the identity of the word. In language it is the sphoṭa that is the real object of utterance, though the form is that of the sounds themselves. This exclusive importance to sphoṭa anticipates in a way the insistence of Firth on saying that the objective of linguistics is 'to make statements of meaning' (see Chapter III).

The later grammarians discussed different varieties of sphoṭa making the distinctions on different parameters:

(i) varṇa sphoṭa (of the letter/sound).
(ii) pada sphoṭa (of the word).
(iii) vākyajāti sphoṭa (of the sentence).

The Naiyāyikas believed that a particular instance of a letter, a word, or a sentence is transient and that we have to bring in the notion of universal 'class' (jati). Viewed from this angle we get the following:

(i) varṇajāti sphoṭa
(ii) padajāti sphoṭa
(iii) vākyajāti sphoṭa.

On the other hand Mīmāṃsakas held the view that the śabda (utterance) is not transient but permanent. Viewed from this angle we get:

(i) varṇavyakti sphoṭa
(ii) padavyakti sphoṭa
(iii) vākyavyakti sphoṭa.

Ānandavardhana followed in the footsteps of Bhartṛhari and developed his theory of **vyañjana** or suggestion. For him 'artha' (meaning) includes not only the cognitive, logical meaning but also emotive elements and the socio-cultural significance of utterances which are suggested with the help of contextual factors.

1.1.1 The Apoha Theory

Another very important theory of meaning the ancient India propounded and developed was the Buddhist theory of *apoha*. According to this theory a positive statement comprises the particular (A) qualified by the negation of the other individuals and discrimination from the class of dissimilar instances. The syllogistic formula of this theory as given by Ratnakirti is as follows:

Major Premise: Whatsoever is a denotative term (implies) the cognition of the mere positive thing A, differentiated from non-A in the judgemental construction.

Example: The statement 'there is water here in this well' distinctly expresses the well, and thus differentiates it from old and dried wells and also from waters in 'non-wells'.

Reason: The reason is identity: "This term 'well' is said to be denotative just as the word 'cow', etc., are (denotative of their objects)."

Conclusion: Thus it is established that every denotative term denotes the positive thing qualified by the discrimination of others in the judgemental construction (Sharma, 1969: 95-97).

This theory, the authors think, has many valuable points which anticipate modern linguistics and psycholinguistics. A detailed discussion of the theory can be found in Sharma (1969), Kunjunni Raja (1963: 78-95) Pandeya (1963: 200-19) and Krishnaswamy *et al.* (2013).

The Buddhist logicians put forward several arguments in favour of their theory (Kunjunni Raja, 1963: 83-84):

(a) Similarity between absolutely dissimilar can be established only by the common exclusion of their counter-correlates.

(b) Anything that can be alternately affirmed or denied is necessarily of the nature of exclusion of its counter-correlates.

(c) The meaning of a word is directly experienced as something distinct, something whose essence consists in the negation of its counter-correlates.

These views can be correlated with the concept of progressive differentiation or discrimination children use while grasping their environment and while picking up language. For example, in the early stages of 'learning how to mean' (cf. Halliday, 1973) children use a word like 'cow' for cows, bullocks and buffaloes. Later on the bullocks and buffaloes are bracketed with non-cows and the cows proper are identified as such. In other words, ***identification implies differentiation.***

1.1.2 Modern Reflections of the Apoha Theory

Firth (1935: 26) says that de Saussure's view that there are only differences in language without positive terms may be due to the possibility of his having learnt something of Indian philosophy. Coming to the Firthian concept of 'system' one is tempted to say it captures the apoha theory in a nutshell. Referring to the use of sixteen vowels in the phonetic context of initial b and final d Firth says that "the phonetic function of each one of the sixteen vowels in that context is its use in contradistinction from fifteen others" (1935: 20). This concept has been fully exploited by Firth, Halliday and several other linguists. The meaning of a term in a system is said to depend on the exclusion of the other terms in the system. For example the meaning of the category 'plural' in the system of number depends on how many other members there are in the system. 'Plural' has certainly different values in the following systems:

1. $\left\{ \begin{array}{l} \text{Singular} \\ \text{Plural} \end{array} \right\}$

2. $\left\{ \begin{array}{l} \text{Singular} \\ \text{Dual} \\ \text{Plural} \end{array} \right\}$

If one views the word from the psychological standpoint the Buddhist theory of apoha explains how we look at the world in terms of opposition, relativity, exclusion, inclusion, differentiation, elimination, etc. (see also Prakasam, 1985: 87-94.)

1.1.3 The Linguistic Event

The Indian view of a linguistic event has been summarized by Kunjunni Raja as follows:

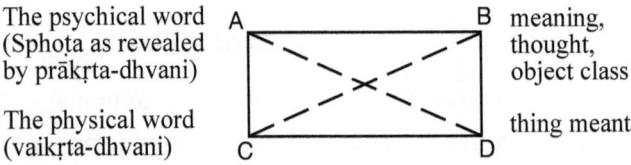

The psychical word A   B meaning,
(Sphoṭa as revealed   thought,
by prākṛta-dhvani)   object class

The physical word   thing meant
(vaikṛta-dhvani)   C   D

Bhartṛhari seems to postulate three stages of speech revelation—*paśyanti, madhyama* and *vaikhari*—corresponding respectively to *sphoṭa, prākṛta dhvani* and *vaikṛta-dhvani*. Sphoṭa, as has already been discussed, is the stage where the whole utterance is considered as one integral unit and this reveals the meaning which is in the form of an intuition (Kunjunni Raja, 1963: 14-15; cf. Brough, 1951: 45).

1.1.4 The Sentence

Before going into some details of the semantic study of words by ancient Indian linguists let us have a look at one of the definitions of sentence given by them:

"that which has no requirement or expectation of word from outside itself to complete its meaning" (Brough, 1953: 162).

The properties constituting the bases of syntactic unity and which are necessary for us to know the meaning of sentence are *ākāṅkṣā* **(syntactic expectancy)** *yogyatā* (logical consistency), *āsatti* or *saṃnidhi* (phonetic contiguity) and *tātparya* (the intention of the speaker or the general purport of the sentence). These aspects of a sentence have been very cogently discussed in Brough (1953) and Kunjunni Raja (1963) and here we present their explication very briefly:

(i) Ākāṅkṣā is the desire or requirement of an individual word or words in the sentence for others to complete the meaning, the factor which distinguishes a sentence from a string of words (cf. collocation, colligation, etc.).

(ii) Yogyatā is the logical compatibility or consistency of the words in a sentence for mutual association. It involves a judgement on the truth or falsity of a statement, or the sense and nonsense of a sentence. (Here we have to agree with Kumārila Bhaṭṭa when he says that incompatibility with the actual facts does not prevent verbal comprehension, but only the validity of the knowledge.)

(iii) 'Āsatti' or 'saṃnidhi' is generally taken to mean the condition that the words in a sentence should be contiguous in time. This contiguity of words leads to contiguity of meanings and finally helps us realize their internal syntactic relationship.

(iv) 'Tātparyajñāna' refers to the general knowledge of the meaning *intended* which is an essential factor in all cases of verbal comprehension (cf. 'intention' in pragmatics).

1.1.5 The Tātparya

The Mīmāṃsakas refer to six *lingas (indications)* which help us get at the tātparya (the message) of a passage without any reference to the speaker or the author, These lingas are:

(a) consistency in meaning through the passage
(b) repetition of the burden of the passage
(c) novelty of the subject matter
(d) result intended
(e) corroborative and eulogistic remarks as distinguished from the main theme
(f) arguments in favour of the main topic.

When we talk about the meaning of a sentence or a passage the question crops up about the phenomenon of ellipsis. The incomplete sentences are said to be of two kinds: (i) 'adhyāhāra', where the sentence is *syntactically incomplete* and requires the supply of the necessary *word,* and (ii) vākyaśeṣa, where the *idea* is incomplete or understood. But Bhartṛhari rejects the very possibility of having elliptical sentences. He says that if a sentence can in a particular context express the meaning required, one should not consider it elliptical.

1.1.6 Uddeśya and Vidheya

Both Naiyāyikas and Mīmāmsakas analysed a sentence into two parts: ***uddeśya and vidheya*** which are anticipatory of the Hallidayan concepts of 'Given' and 'New':

(1) *Uddeśya:* that which is already existent and is known from other sources (siddha); this information is available for both the speaker and the listener.

(2) *Vidheya:* that which is to be brought into existence; this information is available only with the speaker.

These two units give us the informational value of different parts of a sentence. Unfortunately some people have treated them as equivalent to subject-predicate pair or topic-comment pair. As we have already noted, they are equivalent to the concepts of 'Given' and 'New' which were introduced by Halliday (1957) and further developed in his theory of Systemic Grammar (see Halliday, 1967-68, 1967a, 1976 and also Prakasam, 1970, 1979 and 1985; see also Chafe, 1970, 1976).

1.1.7 The Meaning of Words

We shall now briefly survey the views of ancient Indians on the meanings of words. A word is significant in a language because of its significative power. According to Mīmāṃsakas this power is inherent in the words themselves. This theory of natural relationship between a word and its meaning is rejected by the Naiyāyikas and Vaiśeṣikas who advocate the conventional origin of their relationship. All the schools of thought of India however seem to have accepted the functional view of meaning that 'vṛtti' or the function of a word is its relation to the sense.

1.1.8 Learning Word Meanings

We learn the meanings of words in eight different ways:

(i) *vṛddha vyavahāra* (the usage of words by elders) is one of the ways of learning meaning through (a) direct perception (pratyakṣa), (b) inference (anumāna), and (c) postulation (arthapatti);

(ii) *āptavākya* (the direct statement of a trustworthy authority) is another way by which people generally understand the meanings of words;

(iii) *vyākaraṇa* (grammar) helps us with the meanings of the roots, suffixes and derivatives;
(iv) *upamāna* (analogy) is the process of identifying an object with the help of description of an object already known;
(v) *kośa* (lexicon) gives us the primary significative power of words; it may also give the metaphorical senses sanctioned by usage;
(vi) *vākyaśeṣa* (the rest of the passage in the context) comes into the picture when there is a doubt about the meaning of a word (context);
(vii) *vivṛti* (the explanation given by a commentator) determines the meaning of a word, especially in case of doubt;
(viii) *siddhapada sānnidhya* (the syntactic connection of a word with words already known) is yet another way of 'knowing' its meaning.

1.1.9 Synonyms, Homonymy and Contextual Categories

The Sanskrit grammarians and lexicologists discussed the phenomena of synonymy and homonymy. According to them exact synonyms are rare as there are always shades of difference in the meanings of the so-called synonyms. In the case of homonyms some of them advocated *eka śabda darśana* (one-word theory) (homonymy) while some others advocated *aneka śabda darśana* (many words theory) (homophony). The importance of contextual factors was recognized in determining the exact meaning of an expression. Bhartṛhari mentions fourteen different contextual factors:

(1) *saṃsarga* (contact) or *saṃyoga* (association) is a connection that is generally known to exist between two things. A word with several meanings will yield singular interpretation if its habitual association with other words is taken into consideration (e.g. cow with its calf);

(2) *viprayoga* (dissociation) is the disappearance of the connection that is known to exist between two things (e.g. cow without its calf);
(3) *sāhacarya* (companionship) is mutual association as in a compound (e.g. Rama (Srirama) and Lakshmana; Rama (Balarama) and Krishna);
(4) *virodhita* (opposition or well known hostility) between referents may decide the exact interpretation of a given expression (e.g. Rama and Ravana);
(5) *artha* (the purpose served) is another feature of choosing one of the several meanings of a given word;
(6) *prakaraṇa* (the context of situation) helps us disambiguate an expression in several cases;
(7) *linga* (indication) is an indication from another place—another word in the same sentence or in another sentence in the same passage;
(8) *śabdasyanyasya saṃnidhi* (the vicinity of another word) may also restrict the possible meanings of a word (this is similar to 1-4 and 7);
(9) *sāmarthya* (the capacity that is known from the result) is another feature to restrict the meaning of a polysemic expression (this is similar to 5);
(10) *auciti* (the propriety or congruity) may decide the exact meaning of an expression (this is similar to 5);
(11) *deśa* (the place) may sometimes decide the specific meaning of the expression (this is similar to 6);
(12) *kāla* (the time) of an utterance may also restrict the meaning of a polysemic expression (this is similar to 6);
(13) *vyakti* (the grammatical gender) of a word may decide its meaning too (we may extend this argument to other grammatical categories also);

(14) *svara* (the accent) also may decide the correct interpretation of an expression (this we can extend to all the prosodic aspects of the phonological structure of an expression).

1.1.10 Classification of Contextual Categories

All these fourteen factors can easily be reorganized into:
   (i) context, collocation
   (ii) context of situation
   (iii) propriety in terms of purpose, capacity, etc.
   (iv) grammatical properties
   (v) phonological properties.

It is significant to note that Firth uses all these features in his theory of meaning.

1.1.11 Word and Sentence

The controversy about the status of a word in a sentence in terms of meaning can be seen reflected in the two arguments, the *anvitābhidāna vāda* and the *'abhihitānvaya vāda,* put forth by the Prabhākara school and the Bhaṭṭa school respectively (Kunjunni Raja, 1963: 189-222). The former, while recognizing word as the real and actual constituent of language, says that the sentence is the 'integrated meaning of a series of words'. The latter school says that a sentence is 'a series of expressed word meanings'. The Prabhākara school holds the opinion that both the individual word meanings and their mutual relations are conveyed by the words themselves. The Bhaṭṭa school, thinks that the words convey only the individual word meanings and the mutual relation is conveyed by the word meanings, and not by the words. To Bhartṛhari, the sentence meaning is grasped as a unity and words for him are in fact unreal and are only the artificial constructions of the grammarians.

1.1.12 The Primary Meaning of a Word

We wind up our brief survey of diverse Indian theories of meaning by referring to their divergent views about the primary meaning of a word. The divergence centres upon three concepts:

(i) vyakti (the particular)
(ii) ākṛti (the generic shape or form)
(iii) jāti (the universal).

For some scholars (Naiyāyikas of the old school) a word means all the three. For some (Naiyāyikas of the modern school) the primary meaning of a word is particular as characterized by both the universal and the form. For the Sānkhyas and some of the modern Naiyāyikas, it is the percept of the particular, and for the Jain philosophers it is the shape. The Mīmaṃsakas take the primary meaning of a word to be the universal. Bhartṛhari says that every word, first of all, means the class of that word (universal of the form meant). Later it is superimposed on the universal of the 'thing meant'.

1.2.0 Pre-Modern European Tradition: The Modistae

Now let's turn very briefly to some theoretical views about meaning expressed in the Pre-Modern European tradition. In this context two traditions are important: the Modistae (13th and 14th centuries) and the Port Royal theory of 17th century (see Bursill-Hall 1971).

The Modistae of speculative grammar belongs to the period of scholastic philosophy in Europe (1200-1350). Roger Bacon made a very significant statement which anticipates universalist attitudes of the modern linguists. He declared that grammar is one and the same in all languages in its substance, and the surface differences between them are merely accidental variations.

The Modistae were firmly on the side of convention in the physis-nomos (nature-convention) dispute and analogy in the analogy-anomaly controversy. They replaced the formal aspects of the earlier definitions of parts of speech with specific meaning categories. For example, Priscian of sixth century defined 'participium' as

> derivationally referable to verbs sharing the categories of verbs and nouns (tenses and cases), and therefore distinct from both.

Thomas of Erfurt (c 1350) defined 'participium' as

> a part of speech signifying through the mode of temporal process, not separated from the substance (of which it is predicated).

Their contribution to syntax is most significant. An acceptable sentence arises from four principles:

(1) *Material:* The words as members of grammatical classes.
(2) *Formal:* Their union in various constructions.
(3) *Efficient:* The grammatical relations between different parts of speech expressed in the inflexional forms *(modi significandi)* that are required by the construction and imposed by the speaker's mind.
(4) *Final:* The expression of complete thought.

Acceptability requires *three* conditions to be satisfied:

(a) the word classes must be such as to constitute a syntactic construction (e.g. noun and verb);
(b) the words must exhibit appropriate inflexional categories;
(c) the words as individual lexical items must be collocable.

Some of the speculative grammarians adopted a moderate stand on the opposition of realist-nominalist points of view and held that as far as human knowledge is concerned, universals are abstracted from real properties of particulars and then considered apart from them by the mind. In modistic terms the mind abstracts the *modi essendi* from things, considers them as *modi intelligendi,* and language permits such abstractions to be communicated by means of the *modi significandi.*

1.2.1 Port Royal Theory

A very important aspect of the Port Royal theory concerns the philosophical discussion of propositions in terms of *conceiving, judging* and *reasoning.* For example, three judgements are said to pass through one's mind when one says the sentence (Rieux and Rollin, 1975: 99):

Invisible God created the visible world.

The three judgements are:

(a) That *God is invisible.*

(b) That *He created the world.*

(c) That The *world is visible.*

(a) and (c) are considered subordinate propositions and (b) the principal one. Sometimes the subordinate propositions are expressly designated as in relativized constructions such as

God who is invisible created the world which is visible.

It is very important to note that the transformational treatment of attributive constructions is directly traceable to the Port Royal treatment of the phenomenon. It has rightly been stated that the distinction between Deep structure and Surface structure is important in the Cartesian tradition and of course in the Transformational Generative Grammar. It is fair to say that the latter is reminiscent of the former.

Similarly the treatment of the concepts of 'affirmation' and 'negation' in Port Royal grammar anticipates very significantly the treatment of performative verbs (Rieux and Rollin, 1975: 127- 28). For example, the sentence 'Peter affirms' is said to signify two affirmations:

I affirm +

Peter affirms.

Exponents of Port Royal theory asserted the claims of human reason above authority and they made Descartes rather than Aristotle the basis of their teaching. They envisaged a general grammar underlying the actual make-up of all languages. Benazee, the author of a later general grammar, believed that grammar had two sorts of principles—universal, arising from the nature of human thought, and particular, mutable conventions that constitute the grammars of particular languages. The Transformationalist stand on this aspect is basically the same.

CHAPTER II
The Recent Trends

2.1.0 Various Approaches to Recent Trends

Now we shall try to review some of the known trends in the study of meaning in linguistic tradition. In this tradition we shall discuss the following approaches:

   (i) Katz-Fodor approach
  (ii) Weinreich approach
 (iii) Generative Semantics: Lakoff and McCawley
 (iv) Generative Semantics: Chafe
  (v) Fillmore's case grammar
 (vi) Chomsky approach (1965, 1970, 1976, 1981)
(vii) Shaumyan's approach
(viii) Pragmatic approach.

2.1.1 Katz-Fodor Approach

The first assumption Katz and Fodor (1963) make in line with the transformationalist approach to linguistics is as follows:

> The speaker's knowledge of his language takes the form of rules which project the *finite* set of sentences he has fortuitously encountered to the *infinite* sentences of the language.

The second assumption they make is that a fluent speaker's ability consists in the following:

   (i) he can detect non-syntactic ambiguities and characterize the content of each reading of a sentence;
  (ii) he can determine the number of readings a sentence has by exploiting semantic relations in the sentence to eliminate potential ambiguities;

(iii) he can detect semantic anomalies;
(iv) he can paraphrase utterances.

To Katz and Fodor a sentence cannot have readings in a *setting* which it does not have in *isolation*. Hence a semantic interpretation is logically prior to a theory of the selective effect of the setting. The first kind of theory of setting selection seeks to account for the way in which the different aspects of the socio-physical world control the understanding of sentences. The second kind of realization of the abstract formulation of a theory of setting selection is one in which the setting of an occurrence of a sentence is construed as the written or spoken discourse of which the occurrence is a part.

The semantic component of a description of a language interprets the underlying phrase-markers in terms of meaning. To achieve this Katz and Fodor postulate two sub-components within the semantic component:

(a) a dictionary of lexical items of the language, and
(b) the projection rules which operate on full grammatical description of sentences and on dictionary entries to produce semantic interpretation for every sentence of the language.

The meaning of any syntactically compound constituent of a sentence is obtained as a function of the meanings of the parts of the constituent (Katz, 1966: 152). This view is similar to 'abhihitānvaya vāda' which has been referred to above. (See 1.1.11.)

2.1.2 Conceptual Relations

The meanings of words are composed of certain concepts in certain relations. Some of these relations are:

(1) phonological or graphological representation of the word

(2) syntactic markers (noun, verb, etc.)
(3) lexical readings
(4) semantic markers (human, physical, etc.)
(5) selectional restrictions.

The mode of expressing semantic generalizations is the assignments of readings containing the relevant semantic marker(s) to those linguistic constructions over which the generalizations hold and only those. Katz gives useful explanation for the concepts used in the theory (1966: 158-64):

Semantic ambiguity occurs when an underlying structure contains ambiguous word or words that contribute its or their multiple senses to the meaning of the whole sentence, thus enabling that sentence to be used to make more than one statement, request, query, etc.

Semantic anomaly is the limiting case of exclusion by the operation of selection restrictions. Semantically anomalous sentences 'occur when the meanings of the component words of a sentence are such that they cannot combine to form a coherent and directly intelligible sentence'.

There is a distinct projection rule for each distinct grammatical relation. The adequacy of a dictionary entry or a projection rule depends on how well it plays its role within the overall descriptive system (Katz, 1966: 175).

2.1.3 Katz's Views of a Semantic Theory

Here we bring in what Katz has discussed in his Semantic Theory (1972). According to him a semantic theory is expected to explain synonymy and paraphrase, semantic similarity and semantic difference, antonymy, superordination and subordination, meaninglessness and semantic anomaly, semantic ambiguity, semantic redundancy, analytic truth, contradictoriness, syntheticity, inconsistency, entailment, presupposition, possible answer and self-answered question (1972: 6-7).

Katz refers to Frege's principle of 'effability' which is explicated as follows:

> anything which is thinkable is communicable through some sentence of a natural language (because the structure of sentences mirrors the structure of thought) (p. 19).

'Effability' is said to lead us to the basis for an interlinguistic notion of proposition on which can be based the hypotheses about the relation of logic and language.

Katz proposes 'semantic redundancy rules' which are part of the dictionary besides the list of dictionary entries (lexical items). These rules simplify the formulation of dictionary entries by allowing us to eliminate any semantic markers from a lexical reading whose occurrence is predictable on the basis of the occurrence of another semantic marker in the same reading (1972: 44, cf. 1966: 233). The more abstract features leading to less abstract features are left out of the description of individual lexical items (1972: 100). For example, the feature 'animal' need not be accompanied by the feature 'physical' and the feature 'vehicle' need not be accompanied by the feature 'artefact'. This gives us the redundancy rules:

$$\begin{array}{l}\text{(a) (animal)} \\ \text{(b) (vehicle)} \\ \text{(c) (artefact)}\end{array} \left\{\begin{array}{l}\text{(physical)} \\ \text{(artefact)} \\ \text{(object)}\end{array}\right\}$$
$$\text{(physical)}$$
$$\text{(non-living)}$$

Katz gives the following features to describe 'bachelor' (pp. 74, 149):

Bachelor—(human, male, adult, unmarried)

The features 'living' and 'physical' are not brought in because they come under redundancy features. The feature 'human' can predict them. McCawley makes a further distinction among the non-redundancy features: (actual) meaning feature and (selection restriction) presupposition feature (1968: 267). Then the word bachelor can be represented as follows:

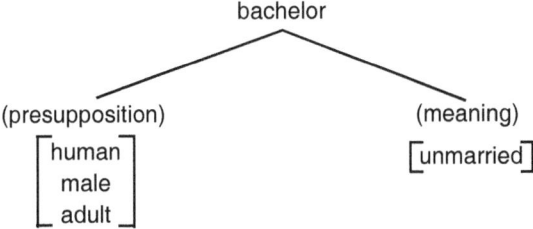

Katz objects to this approach and reserves the concept 'presupposition' only for sentential level. This terminological (or conceptual) commitment does not seem to be justifiable. Zuber supports McCawley's distinction and calls the 'meaning' features 'asserted' features (1972). We have hitherto discussed the nature of the semantic component of Generative Syntax. By bringing in the concept of presupposition discussed by McCawley we are on the threshold of Generative Semantics.

2.2.1 Weinreich's Model: The Lexical Entry

According to Weinreich (1966: 417) a lexical entry may be considered a triplet: a set of phonological features (P), a set of syntactic features (G), and a set of semantic features (M). He believes that ambiguity belongs to surface structure and that the deep structure is free of it (418). To ensure that, he stipulates that a lexical entry be so defined that its component

M—the set of its semantic features—is free of disjunctions. He defines two kinds of semantic features: *configurations* (ordered features), and *clusters* (unordered features). The features which form a configuration must be taken in the set order.

For example, if one assigns for *'chair'* the features 'furniture' and 'sitting', they should be taken in that order only and not the other way. But on the other hand the features which form a cluster can be taken in any order (419). If the two features for 'daughter' are 'offspring' and 'female' they can be taken in any order. If all types of combination of features of the constituents in a construction combine to form a cluster, the construction is called linking. If they do not form a cluster, the construction is called non-linking (420).

2.2.2 Linking

Linking must be understood as capable of taking place on several levels at the same time. Weinreich proposes an instance of linking in the following analysis where (a) = wall, (b) = white, and (c) = astonishing (422):

(b) = ... white ... = the white one
(a, b) = the wall is white = ...the white wall...
(a, c) = the wall is astonishing = ... the astonishing wall...
(a, bc) = the wall's whiteness is astonishing
(b, c) = the white one is astonishing
(,bc) = whiteness is astonishing
(a, cb) = the wall is astonishingly white = astonishingly white wall.

The non-linking constructions are of three kinds:

(1) *Nesting:* A nesting construction does not produce any new cluster of features. If M(a) and N(c) are words with their semantic features, and if MN is a construction, its semantic effect is described as nesting if it yields the configuration (a-c), e.g. buy flowers (p. 424).

(2) *Delimination:* This construction effects restriction of the class of referents of a sign, e.g. to convert the general sheep into *same sheep, these sheep, into five sheep, one sheep, etc.* (pp. 426-27).

(3) *Modalization:* This can be as an instruction to interpret a particular semantic entity with some classification. Sentence adverbials and conjugational modes seem to fall into this group (p. 428).

2.2.3 Transfer Feature

It is common to find that when two lexical items cooccur, the semantic feature of one is transferred to the other. For example 'craft' gets specified as 'water-craft' if it occurs with 'to sail'. This phenomenon is called the 'transfer feature'. Therefore the lexical item 'to sail' has a transfer feature, say, 'water vehicle', as distinguished from 'to operate' which does not have the transfer feature. Weinreich discusses the distinct advantages of imposing a syntactic form on the semantic features contained in the dictionary, i.e., by formulating them into definitions. Such a step would make it possible to represent certain sets of sentences as paraphrases of each other. He remarks that idioms should be listed in the dictionary together with their syntactic structure instead of being treated merely as words'. Furthermore each of the constituents of an idiom should be itemized with full dictionary entries (P.G.M.).

Weinreich's approach discussed above paves the way of the Generative Semantics approach of McCawley, Lakoff, Ross and others.

2.3.0 Generative Semantics: Lakoff, McCawley *et al.*

'Generative Semantics' has been offered as an improvement on Generative Syntax. Seuren (1971) in fact prefers a different set of terms to refer to these two different approaches of transformational grammar. The former he calls 'semantic syntax' and the latter 'autonomous syntax'. The semantic syntax approach argues that the semantic structure is the structure from which should emanate the syntactic structure. The semantic structure cannot be given the status of being an 'interpreted output' but should be treated as the 'structurating input'. In this approach the semantic structure is given as a set of structures with semantic features as the constituents. These features are later replaced by lexical items by the lexical insertion transformations. The lexical items are not inserted in one block. They are inserted at different stages of the derivation of the structure. We therefore get pre-lexical and post-lexical transformations. The generative or autonomous syntax model envisages the insertion of all the lexical items in one block. So the lexically specified structure is considered the deep structure. Semantic syntax questions the need to have such a deep structure as a recognizable unit. As we proceed now it would be clear that linguists of Generative Syntax and Generative Semantics were too engrossed in the accurate formalism to go deep into the nuances of word-meaning and sentence-meaning. (For a detailed criticism of the two models see Bartsch and Vennemann, 1972: 6-28.)

2.3.1 Salient Features of Generative Semantics

Some idea of the approach adopted for the study of meaning in Generative Semantics can be had by examining the following sentence:

1. John would have been protesting.

In the earlier analyses of transformational grammar tense, modality, perfective, and progressive were analysed as constituents of the auxiliary. The Generative Semantics approach analysed each auxiliary verb as a separate semantico-syntactic unit within the verb phrase. The abstract representation of 1 is

1'. The affix transformation operates to produce the intermediate structure:

John do will-past have be-en protest-ing.

The presence of *do* in underlying structure obviates the need for a *do* transformation and makes *do* automatically available for questions and negative sentences. But now a transformation is required to delete *do* when it is not followed by a tense affix.

John will-past have be-en protest-ing.

This is converted to 1.

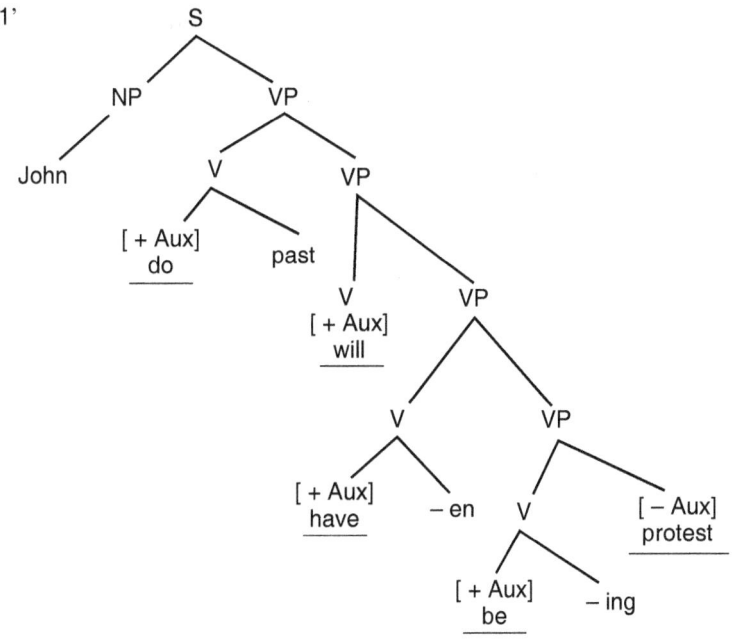

It is to be noted that all auxiliaries and regular verbs are marked [+ V] and auxiliaries are further assigned a syntactic feature [+ Aux]. Hence Ross's argument had been that auxiliary verbs are, in deep structure, main verbs taking sentential complements. Other than the question of auxiliary, many other constituents of surface clauses (e.g. adverbs, quantifiers, negation) have also been analysed as the predicates of higher clauses at the level of deep structure posited by Generative Semantics (thus deriving single clause from two clauses in the deep structures). For example, Lakoff (1965) observed that the question (2) and the negative sentence (3) both presuppose that some wife-beating has been occurring, and that they are synonymous respectively with the two-clause sentences (4) and (5).

2. Do you beat your wife enthusiastically?
3. You don't beat your wife enthusiastically.
4. Are you enthusiastic in beating your wife?
5. You are not enthusiastic in beating your wife.

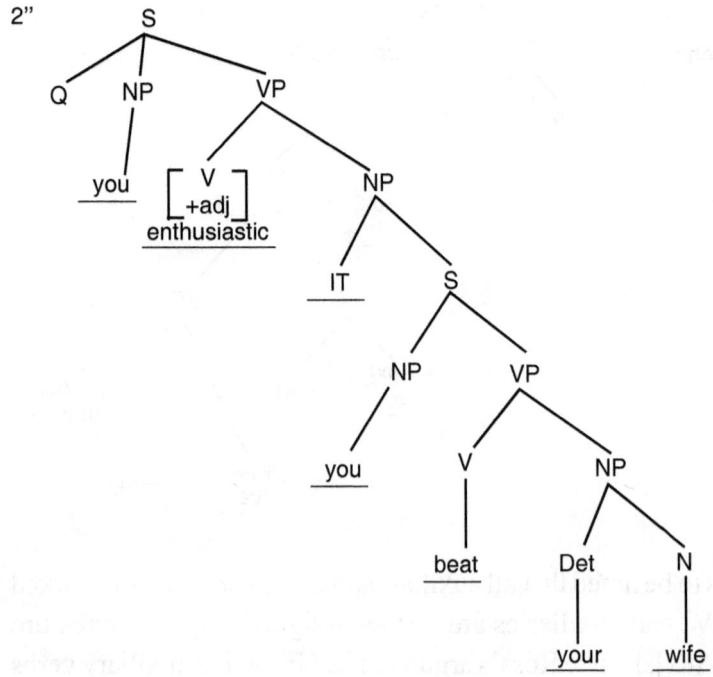

What is questioned and negated in (2) and (3) is the adverb *only*; the scope of the question and the negation is not the whole sentence or verb phrase. The deep structure tree of 2 will not only capture the paraphrasal relationship between the one-clause sentence (2) and the two-clause sentence (4) but also the scope restriction of the question. This two-clause deep structure, which is what underlies the two-clause sentence (4), is thus claimed also to underlie the one-clause sentence. To derive the latter, an optional adverb-lowering transformation is needed that will move the higher verb down as an adverb in the subordinate clause, and delete the remainder of the main clause.

2.3.2 Category Distinctions

Another important feature of Generative Semantics had been the breakdown of traditional category distinctions. Nouns, verbs, adjectives, prepositions, all partially overlap in their syntactic behaviour. It was felt that if two or more traditional classes are combined into one general class with their differences being marked by different syntactic features, generalization of transformation can be achieved. For example, Lakoff (1965) proposes that verbs and adjectives should be classified as members of a single-category Verb, differentiated by the features [+ Adj] and [— Adj]. Consider (6) and (7) which are synonymous, differing only in the category of their predicates.

    6. John considers Mary's feelings.
    7. John is considerate of Mary's feelings.

The grammatical relations between *John* and *considers* and between *John* and *is considerate* are intuitively the same, as are those between *considers* and *Mary's feelings* and *is considerate of* and *Mary's feelings*. The selection restrictions on the subjects and objects of these predicates are also alike: *Mary,* for example, can be the subject of neither. To capture these similarities, Lakoff proposed assigning pairs of sentences like (6) and (7) deep structures identical except for the feature [± Adj]. The two sentences have virtually the same deep structure, which exhibits some of the properties of each of the two distinct surface sentences. This difference between the two is treated as superficial difference, introduced in the course of the transformational derivation and represented by only single feature at the deep structure level.

It has also been observed (Bach, 1968) that predicate nominals also share properties with adjectives and verbs.

8. The attempt was a failure.
9. The attempt failed.

Predicate nominals like a *failure* share selection restrictions and grammatical relations with verbs; like verbs it must agree with its subject. Hence the deep structure of 8 and 9 will be identical, the difference being captured by transformational derivation. Predicate nominals, in effect, are represented as verbs, thus doing away with the interpretive semantic component.

2.3.3 Differences and Identity of Meaning

Systematic differences in meaning, as well as identity of meaning, have also been captured transformationally in Generative Semantics. For example, many adjectives (e.g. *hard, thick*) have corresponding morphologically related inchoative verbs (harden, thicken).

10. The metal is hard.
11. The metal hardened.
12. The sauce is thick.
13. The sauce thickened.

Hardened and *thickened* are inchoative verbs meaning 'become X'. Lakoff (1965) proposed deriving the inchoative verbs from their corresponding adjectives in the context of *become*. Thus the deep structure for 13 would be 13'.

13'

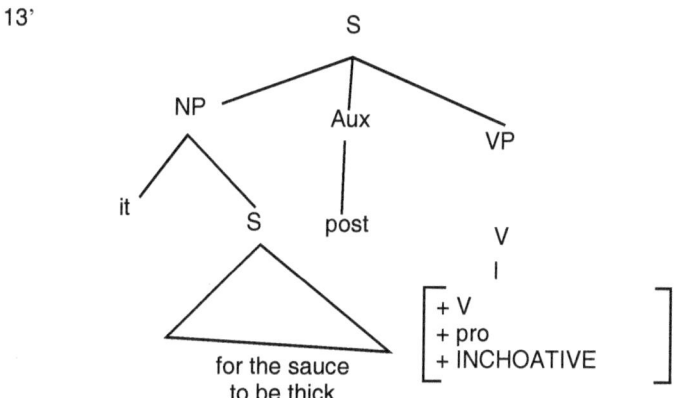

After the application of *subject-raising transformation* we get and intermediate structure 13".

13"

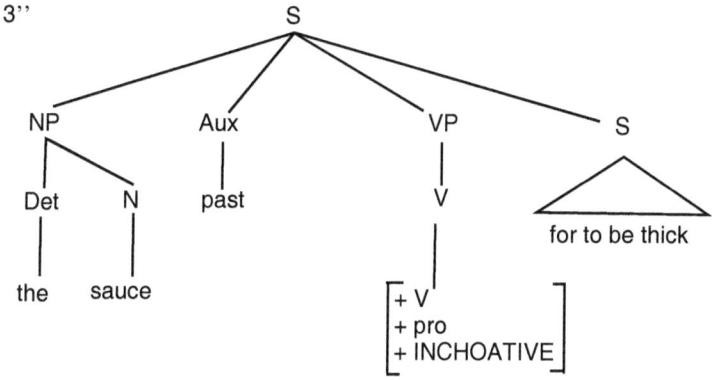

The complementizer *for* and the copula *to be* are deleted, leaving only *thick* under the lower S node. *Inchoative transformation* is then applied to substitute *thick* for the abstract inchoative verb to produce a verb with the feature [+ INCHOATIVE]:

13''''

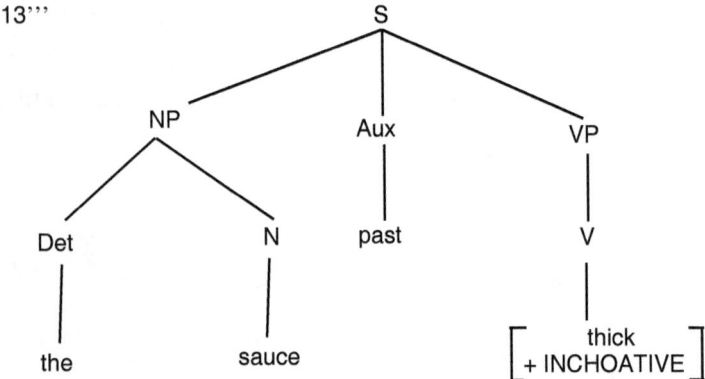

A late 'spelling' rule must then supply the ending -en to *thick*.

A similar analysis was also proposed for causative verbs such as *thicken* in sentence 14.

14. John thickened the sauce.

Here the subject of thicken is agent *John* and the direct object of thicken is *sauce*. (14') exhibits that John caused the sauce to thicken which is represented in the deep structure:

14'

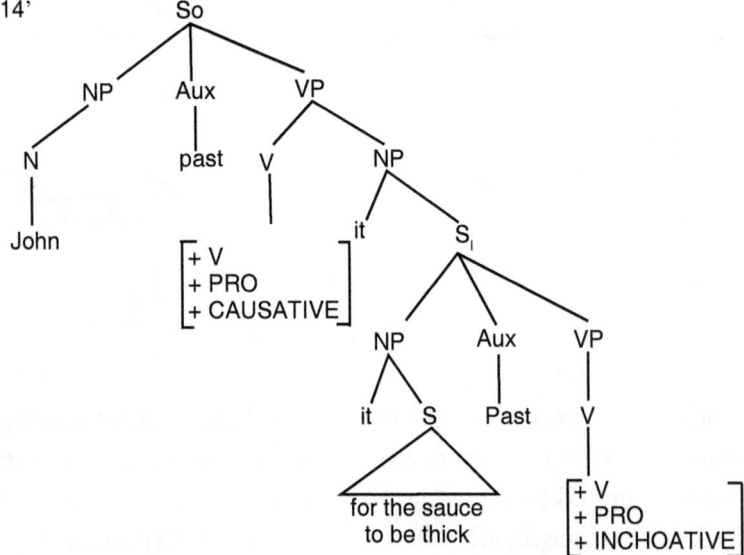

Notice that the complement of the causative verb is the inchoative sentence (13): *the sauce thickened*. After deriving *the sauce thickened* as explained earlier, causative transformation is applied to raise the newly formed *thicken* (inchoative) and substitute it for the abstract Causative Pro-Verb and thereby derives the causative verb *thicken*.

"In this fashion, derivational morphology is accommodated within the syntactic component. The relation between *thick* and *thicken* is determined by deep structures and syntactic transformation and not by special morphological rules in the lexicon" (Fodor, 1977). Such transformations make it possible to derive those causative verbs which have no parallel morphologically related source verbs. This is done by assuming a hypothetical lexical item with certain phonological form. For example, if *kill* means 'cause to die' then *kill* can be derived by the causative transformation from a hypothetical lexical item with the phonological form of *kill* but the meaning and distribution of *die*. Hence *the aspect of the internal semantic analysis of lexical items is captured syntactically* (Fodor, 1977). Sentences 15, 16, 17 would be semantically specified as 15', 16' and 17', respectively.

15. John is dead.　　　15. John is not alive.
16. John died.　　　　16. John became not alive.
17. Jim killed John.　　17. Jim caused John to become not alive.

Surface sentences such as 15, 16, 17 would then be arrived at by predicate-raising transformation followed by insertion of appropriate lexical item. The operation is also known as 'pre-lexical transformation'.

2.3.4 Universal Semantic Elements

In fact, the next step in Generative Semantics was to introduce deep structures that contain no lexical items but universal semantic elements. This move was primarily made by McCawley (1968). A causative sentence 18 would be assigned the deep structure 18'.

18. We killed snakes.

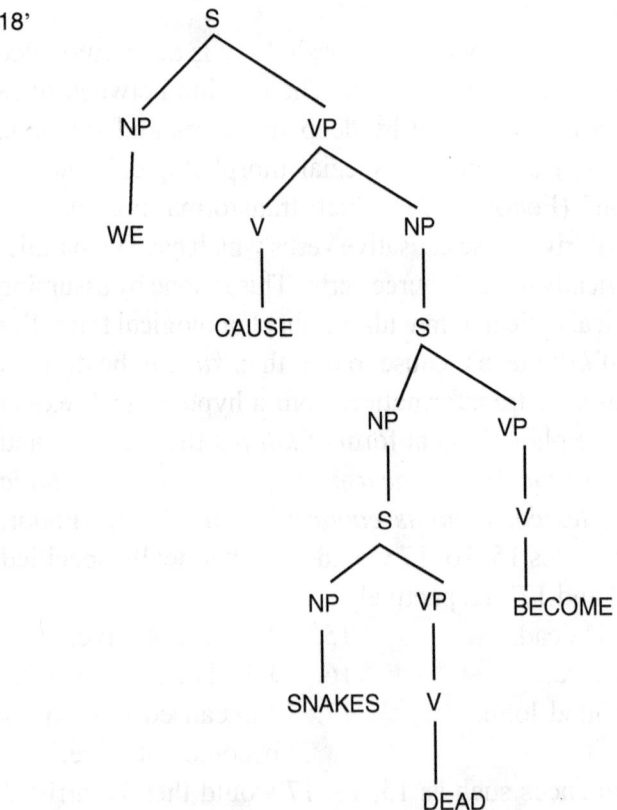

The terminal elements in this phrase-marker are written in capitals to indicate that they are not language-specific lexical items but are universal semantic primitives. Later a general transformation (like predicate-raising) would collect CAUSE, BECOME and DEAD into a single constituent and jointly substitute them by the English lexical item *kill*. Sometimes, however, such general transformations result in a semantic complex which does not correspond to any lexical item in the language. For example, there is no lexical item for BECOME ANGRY in English. For this, predicate-raising will be allowed to apply freely and unlexicalizable products of it will be filtered out by dictionary. In this way, the dictionary provides an automatic filter on derivations.

Once syntactic structures are allowed to contain universal semantic elements as their terminal symbols, the syntactic deep structures of sentences can serve as their semantic representations.

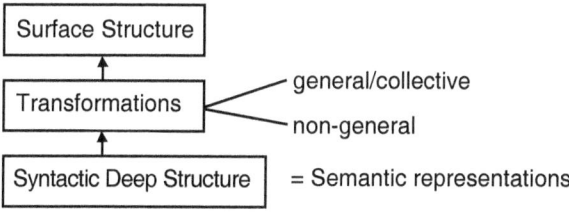

Fig.1: G.S. representation

The interpretive semantic component which was introduced in Generative Syntax model (Chomsky 1965) is now dispensed with entirely—hence the name 'Generative Semantics'.

Generative Semantics admits global rules and derivational constraints (i.e. transformations). Transformations are considered a special case of derivational constraint which happen to be Local. They determine permissible relations between two Adjacent phrase-makers in a derivation. Indeed, Lakoff (1974) and others did not regard Generative Semantics as a variety of transformational grammar.

2.3.5 Recent Developments in Generative Semantics

Later developments in the field of Generative Semantics came a long way and at times it is difficult to pin-point which are the latest contributions. However, some later contributions can be briefly summarized as follows:

    a. It is claimed that many syntactic processes require reference to grammatical relations. For instance, reference is needed to the Subject of a verb rather than merely to the noun phrase which directly precedes the verb. Further, it is claimed that there are universal generalizations about possible types of rules which can be captured only in these terms. Since grammatical relations are very much relevant to semantics, the sharp distinction between syntactic rules and semantic rules is rejected (Postal, 1974; Perlmutter and Postal, 1983).

    b. Ross (1972, 1973a, 1973b, 1974, 1975) developed a 'Squishy' approach to grammar which rejects restrictive assumptions of the standard theory such as 'a constituent must either be a member of a certain category or not'. Category membership is a matter of degree, and different syntactic transformations may differ in the degree of membership they demand. For example, sentences (19) to (22) represent a declining degree of acceptability.

19. It's strange that you are so embarrassed.
20. It's strange for you to be so embarrassed.
21. It's strange you being so embarrassed.
22. It's strange your embarrassment.

Similarly, Lakoff (1972) has applied the theory of 'fuzzy sets' to natural language data. Consider the following sentences:

23. A penguin is a bird.
24. Strictly speaking, a penguin is a bird.
25. A penguin is a bird par excellence.

Instead of assuming that anything must either be a bird or not be a bird, the concept of 'birdiness' is defined by a function which permits degrees of membership in the set of birds. Robins enjoy full membership, chickens and penguins to a lesser degree, and cows don't belong to this group at all. Phrases which Lakoff calls 'hedges' interact with such words and directly exploit their fuzziness. Sentence (23) is claimed to be only partly true, but the hedged sentence (24) is fully true, and the hedged sentence (25) is completely false (Fodor, 1977). Generative Semanticists claimed that facts about the world, about speakers' and hearers' beliefs about the world, about their relative social status, theories dealing with perception and production processes, stylistic preferences, pragmatic constraints of all kinds, and so on, must all be fed into the grammar which determines the form-meaning correlations for the language. With reference to English conjunction 'and', Grice (1981) distinguished between meaning in a strict sense, and pragmatically determined connotations and implications.

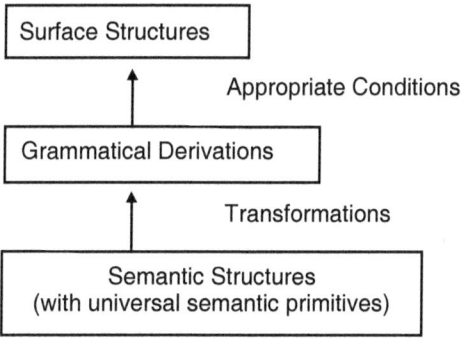

Fig.2: The later position of Generative Semantics

At this point we would be justified in raising a very simple but fundamental issue, viz., "Why do we write grammars"? Obviously to account for what we said at the beginning—to see how languages do what they do, viz., function as systems of communication. This will lead us to have either speaker-oriented grammars or listener-oriented grammars. We can of course have text-based or discourse-based grammars. If these grammars are not to be linked to the encoding or decoding procedures there is no particular need to have transformational grammars with the misleading impression, though not claimed by their adherents, that they capture the generative process of the sentences. What we then need is a text-based grammar telling us how it is structured, how it means what it means and how it is articulated in the 'appropriate' way—appropriate in the sense that the utterance conveys the meaning the sentence is intended to convey. If we accept this what we need is the sentence given as it is and a multi-valued description of it.

The second point to be raised here is the need to establish the semantic features of a word in terms of specific structures, A speaker or hearer 'uses' or 'receives' words as he 'knows' them. We have to evaluate the meaning of the word 'know' here—it is not absolute knowledge. It is not very uncommon to come across situations where we use words more or less appropriately but cannot explain their use adequately. We may, however, say that linguistic knowledge (competence) of at least the common man is essentially unconscious.

2.4.0 Generative Semantics: Chafe

When we want to treat the deep structure as sequence-free semantic features as Chafe (1970) does in his version of Generative Semantics we are on a safer ground. This version of semantic theory claims to be generative in that it tries to capture various processes through which a message passes in order to convert the initial experience, which an individual tries to communicate to another individual, into the actual phonetic utterance. The experiential universe of a speaker of a language is organized in arrangements of semantic units which make up the semantic structure of that system. A set of transformations converts semantic structure into surface structure. Let us look into the Chafian theory in a little detail. (For detailed evaluation of the theory see Bartsch and Vennemann 1972: 28-30.)

2.4.1 Aspects of Chafe's Theory

Chafe asserts that the well-formedness of linguistic utterances is determined in the semantic structure and not in a "fancied deep structure lying somewhere between semantic structure and surface structure" (1970: 65). If a semantic structure is properly put in accordance with the rules of semantic formation which a language dictates, then a well-formed phonetic output is usually assumed. The reverse is clearly not the case.

An account of surface structure for all natural languages must be based on the centrality of the 'verb', the 'verb' being the item which determines the main features of the organization of the rest of the sentence. A verb may be specified in terms of various 'selectional' units (e.g. state, action, etc.) one of whose functions is to narrow the conceptual field until finally a lexical unit, or a verb root (e.g. 'sing', 'laugh', etc.) is chosen as the narrowest concept of all. There may then be further specification of the verb in terms of inflectional units (e.g. perfective, past, etc.). Once the verb is specified in these several ways, its selectional units determine the introduction of (usually) one or more accompanying nouns, in various possible relations to the verb. Each noun is then subject to its own specification in terms of *selectional units* (e.g. animate, human, etc.), a *lexical unit* (e.g. 'boy', 'cat', etc.), and *inflectional units* (e.g. plural, generic, etc.). There is also another kind of semantic unit, called a *derivational unit,* whose function is to convert a particular verb or noun root, having certain intrinsic properties, into a derived lexical unit with different properties.

Chafe (1970: 167) treats the role of selectional units as distinct from that of inflectional units. He proposes that inflectional units do not influence the choice of the lexical unit (as the selectional units do) and *are not* redundant (as the selectional units are) if the lexical unit is known. To quote him, "the presence or absence *of past* has nothing to do with limiting the choice of the lexical unit, nor does the presence of the lexical unit *buy* say anything about whether or not *past* is also present'. It is semantic units like *past* to which I shall give the name *inflectional*. Inflectional units, then *do not* influence the choice of lexical unit and *are not* redundant if the lexical unit is known (authors' emphasis). On the contrary, "the selectional units of a verb have two distinct functions. Operating outside the verb, they dictate the presence of accompanying nouns. Operating inside the verb they limit the choice of a lexical unit, or verb root ... once a lexical unit has been chosen, the selectional units that led to the choice are redundant, for each lexical unit implies by its own presence the concurrent presence of certain combinations of selectional units." This is the reason why Chafe, in the semantic structure description, writes all selectional units above a line and inflectional units below the line. For instance, in the sentence, "The elephant stepped on my car", *elephant* will be specified as follows:

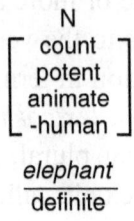

The selectional units like *count, animate, -human* will influence the choice of a noun root like *elephant.* Typically, though not always, inflectional units have some overt surface structure representation. Moreover, since inflectional units are semantic units, besides adding some meaning to a verb they can also influence the inflectional units of the accompanying nouns. Abbi (1975) has also established that at times inflectional units also influence the choice of a verbal lexical unit and in turn the choice of the accompanying noun. She posits a direct relationship between inflectional and selectional units.

Starting from the proposition that language is a way of converting meaning into sound, four distinctly different kinds of processes are involved. First, there are processes of *'formation'* by which a semantic structure is constructed at the outset. Second, there are processes of *'transformation'* by which a semantic structure is modified to become a surface structure. And, third, there are processes of *'symbolization'* by which post-semantic units of a surface representation are replaced by underlying phonological configurations. Finally, there are phonological processes which finally lead to phonetic output. The whole picture would look like the following:

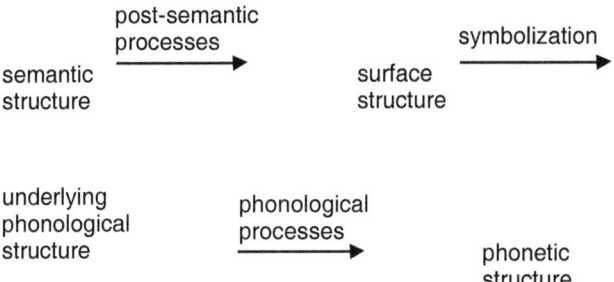

The post-semantic processes consist of first deciding the surface structure subject and object nouns on the basis of semantic units like agent, patient, and experiencer. After this, *agreement* rules are formulated to concord one element with another. Third, the question of *linearization* is considered, its main concern being to spread out the elements along a single dimension which is then *symbolized* by the phonetic dimension of time.

Verbs as introduced by Chafe fall into four main types:
1. State verbs: dry, dead, tight, broken, etc.
2. Process verbs: break, dry, die, tighten (intransitive).
3. Action verbs: laugh, sing, run.
4. Action process verbs: break, dry, kill, tighten (transitive).

Chafe enlists a series of semantic derivational processes by which one form can be derived from another (1970: 119-43). That is, a derivation process called *inchoative* would derive 'widen' (which is a process verb) from the adjective 'wide' (which is a state verb). The derivational units serve as links connecting verbs within one case frame with verbs within another case frame. A derivation process is not free and is subject to some strict conditions. Cook (1972a) has summarized the process diagrammatically as given below:

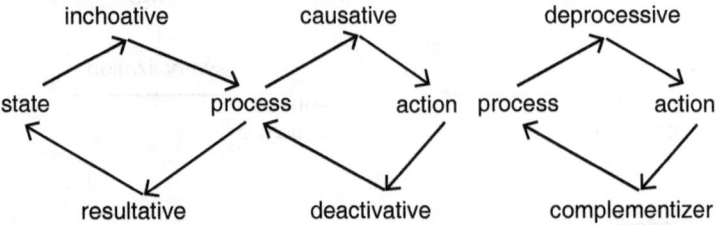

These derivations, as can be seen, form a series of closed loops converting state, process, action process and action verbs. Derivation may proceed from state by inchoative to process, and from process by causative to action process, and from action process by deprocessive to action; or, in the other direction, derivation may proceed from action by complementizer to action process, and from action process by deactivative to process and from process by resultative to state.

2.4.2 Noun-Verb Relations

Besides these four main types of verbs, Chafe has also introduced seven noun-verb relations in his study. They are: *Agent, Experiencer, Benefactive, Patient, Complement, Location* and *Instrument*. All the cases except the instrumental case require a selectional feature in the verb. Cook (1972: 18) has attempted to give a Case Frame Matrix (Table 1) which utilizes the basic verb types and six of the above noun-verb relations. The instrumental case has not been included and patient and complement are grouped into one. Since an action verb is always accompanied by an agent noun/and a state verb by an object/patient noun a separate column is not made for these two noun relations.

Table 1: Case Frame Matrix

A Basic verb types	B + Experiencer	C + Benefactive	D + Locative
1. State	1. State experiencer	1. State benefactive	1. State locative
+ P_s	+ P_s' E	+ B_s' P	+ P_s' L
2. Process	2. Process experiencer	2. Process benefactive	2. Process locative
+ P	+ P' E	+ P' B	+ P' L
3. Action	3. Action** experiencer	3. Action** benefactive	3. Action locative
+ A	+ A' E	+ A' B	+ A' L
4. Action process	4. Action** process experiencer	4. Action process benefactive	4. Action process locative
+ A' P	+ A' P' E	+ A' P' B	+ A' P' L

* All O_s (for object) have been changed to P (for patient).
** Not developed by Chafe.

Cook (1972) developed the case frames which are marked by ** in Table: 1. Some of the examples of A, E are: *frighten, please, answer, question,* etc. and of A, B are: *arm, bribe, help* and *supply.*

It seems necessary to define each of the possible verb types which are listed in Table: 1. The following definitions are the same as presented by Chafe and Cook:

A.1 **State verbs:** A state verb specifies that an object is in a certain state or condition. It is accompanied by a patient noun which specifies what it is that is in that state, e.g. dry, broken.

A.2 ***Process verbs:*** A process verb specifies that an object undergoes a change of state or condition. It is accompanied. by a patient noun which specifies what it is that changes its state or condition, e.g. die, widen.

A.3 ***Action verbs:*** An action verb expresses an activity, something which someone does. It is accompanied by an agent noun which specifies the instigator of the action, e.g. *dance, laugh* and *play.*

A.4 ***Action process verbs:*** An action process verb simultaneously expresses an action and a process. It is accompanied by an agent noun which specifies the instigator of the action and a patient noun which specifies the object effected or affected by that activity, e.g., *build, break, cut.*

B.1 ***State experiencer verb:*** A state experiencer verb specifies that an experiencer is in a certain state or condition with respect to a given object. It is accompanied by an experiencer noun which specifies the one who is in the psychological state of sensation, emotion, cognition. It is also accompanied by a patient noun which specifies the stimulus for or the content of the experience, e.g., *like, want, doubt.*

B.2 ***Process experiencer verbs:*** A process experiencer verb specifies that an experiencer undergoes a change of state with respect to a given object. It is accompanied by an experiencer noun which specifies the one who undergoes the change of psychological state, and a patient noun which specifies the stimulus for or the content of the experience, e.g., *amuse, annoy, please.*

B.3 ***Action experiencer verbs:*** An action experiencer verb expresses *an* activity which results in a change of psychological state for someone else. It is accompanied by an agent noun, which specifies the instigator of the action, an experiencer noun which specifies the one who undergoes the psychological experience, e.g., *congratulate, praise.*

B.4 ***Action process experiencer verbs:*** An action process experiencer verb expresses an activity which places an object as a stimulus or content for someone else's psychological experience. It is accompanied by an agent noun which specifies the instigator of the action, a patient noun which specifies the content or stimulus for the experience, and an experiencer noun which specifies the one who undergoes the psychological experience, e.g., *ask, say, tell.*

C.1 ***State benefactive verbs:*** A state benefactive verb specifies that a benefactor is in a certain state or condition with respect to a given object. It is accompanied by a benefactive noun which specifies the possessor of the object, and a patient noun which specifies the object possessed, e.g., *have,* own.

C.2 ***Process benefactive verbs:*** A process benefactive verb specifies that a benefactor undergoes a change of state or condition with respect to a given object. It is accompanied by a benefactive noun which specifies the one who undergoes gain or loss, and a patient noun which specifies the object which is gained or lost, e.g., *win, lose*.

C.3 ***Action benefactive verbs:*** An action benefactive verb specifies that an agent has caused a gain or loss to a benefactor with respect to a given object. It is accompanied by an agent noun which specifies the cause of the gain or loss, and a benefactive noun which specifies the one who undergoes the gain or loss, e.g., *arm, bribe, supply*.

C.4 ***Action process benefactive verbs:*** An action process benefactive verb specifies that an agent has caused gain or loss to a benefactor with respect to a given object. It is accompanied by an agent noun which specifies the cause of the gain or loss, and a patient noun which specifies the object transferred. For example, *buy, sell, accept*.

D.1 ***State locative verbs:*** A state locative specifies that an object is in a certain location. It is accompanied by a patient noun which specifies what it is that is in that place, and a locative noun which specifies the place where the object is located. For example, *dwell, stay*, etc.

D.2 ***Process locative verbs:*** A process locative verb specifies that an object changes its location. It is accompanied by a patient noun which specifies what it is that has changed its location, and a locative noun which specifies the change of location. For example, *come, go, shift* (with inanimate subjects).

D.3 ***Action locative verbs:*** An action locative verb expresses an activity resulting in change of location. It is accompanied by an agent noun which specifies the instigator of the action, and simultaneously expresses the object being moved when agent and patient are coreferential. It is also accompanied by a locative noun which specifies the change of location. For instance, *fly, run, come, go* (with animate subjects).

D.4 *Action process locative verbs:* An action process locative verb expresses an activity involving the change of place of an object as distinct from the agent. It is accompanied by an agent noun which specifies the instigator of the action, a patient noun which specifies the object which is changing location, and a locative noun which specifies the change of location, for example *bring, put, take, etc.*

It is to be noted that Chafe derives D.2, D.3 and D.4 from intrinsic action, process, and action process verbs, respectively by a derivation called 'locativizer'.

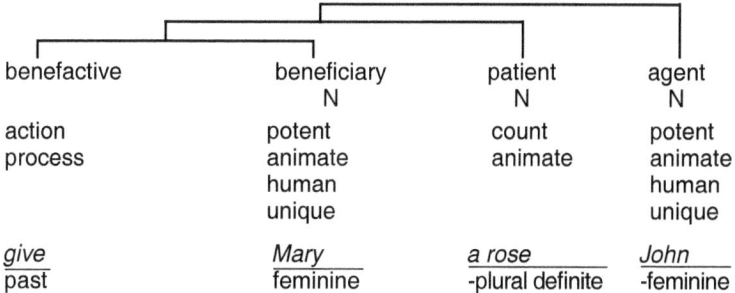

2.4.3 The Semantic Structure of a Sentence

Let us see how a sentence is represented in its semantic structure.

1. John gave a rose to Mary.

It is the verb *give* which chooses the accompanying nouns. Since *give* is a benefactive verb which is also an action process verb, it is accompanied by an agent noun (John) who performs the action of giving, a patient noun—the object (a rose) which changes hands and a beneficiary noun (Mary) to whom the *rose is* given.

Other than the verbs described in the matrix Chafe also considers verbs used in sentences like:

2. It is raining.
3. It is hot.
4. He sang a song.
5. Indians fought the battle.

The first two sentences (2, 3) lack any nouns, considering that it is not the usual anaphoric pronoun referring to some identifiable antecedent. The pronouns in 2 and 3 have no real semantic content. The verbs in these sentences describe either an action which is a part of a natural phenomenon (2) or *a* state which is an all-encompassing state that is not localized in any clearly identifiable noun. Chafe specifies this kind of verbs as Ambient—something which signifies the total environment.

In sentences (4) and (5) the verb describes a certain action which, by its very nature, implies the coexistence of a certain nominal concept. Singing, for example, implies a song; fighting implies a fight or a battle. Hence such a verb involves an action which causes something to be created. Such verbs are called Completable verbs and their nouns are known as Complements. A complement noun does not specify something that is in a state or that changes its state. It completes or specifies more narrowly the meaning of the verb.

So far we have been discussing the nature of noun-verb relations. As stated earlier the inflectional units of nouns and verbs are also semantic units which are chosen after the selection of the lexical unit. Let us consider two of the inflectional units in some detail. One of the very important inflectional units of verb is Generic. Consider the following sentences:

6. John *sings* (= John is a singer).
7. Bob *opens* the door (= Bob is a doorman).
8. The door *opens* (= everytime).

The verbs in these examples communicate a timeless propensity of an indefinite number of events (as explained in parentheses). Any non-state verb can be optionally specified as generic. Moreover, any experiential or benefactive verb regardless of whether it is a state or not can be also specified as generic. Chafe maintains that if a verb is generic it determines the genericness of the *nouns* which accompany it (1970: 189). Thus in the following sentence

9. A bird sings songs.

both the agent and the complement nouns are generic.

2.4.4 Discussion Initiated by Chafe (1974, 1976)

What is more important than this discussion of inflectional units of nouns is the discussion initiated by Chafe (1974, 1976) regarding the ideas expressed by the nouns in the context of the consciousness of the hearer-speaker. In addition to the 'case' status of nouns, they may occupy varying 'packaging' statuses selected by the speaker on the basis of the assessment of what the addressee's mind is capable of at the time. Six such statuses that a noun may have are discussed here:

1. *Given or New:* "Given (or old (1970)) information is that knowledge which the speaker assumes to be in the consciousness of the addressee at the time of the utterance. New information is "what the speaker assumes he is introducing with the addressee's consciousness by what he says". (See also 3.4.1).
2. *Focus of contrast:* the item selected by the speaker from a limited set of possible candidates as the correct choice for the role in question.

3. **Definite:** that item which the speaker assumes that the addressee will identify the referent of.
4. **Subject:** that item about which knowledge is being added.[1]
5. **Topic:** the status which is hard to define in clear-cut terms as at times it overlaps the status of subjecthood. Topics appear to limit the applicability of the main predication to a certain selected domain. In many languages "the topic sets a spatial, temporal, or individual framework within which the main predication holds". (See also Section 3.4.1)
6. **Empathy or point of view:** that is, referent of a noun may be the individual with whom the speaker is empathizing. For instance, in saying *John loved his wife* the speaker is describing the event from John's side, while in saying *Mary's husband loved her* the event is described from Mary's side. The empathy is with *John* and *Mary* respectively. In a typical sentence there cannot be more than one focus of empathy. (See also Section 3.4.1).

2.5.0 Fillmore's Case Grammar (1968)

It postulates a deep structure configuration with a set of noun phrases related to a given verb phrase on specified casal dimensions. In both these versions (Chafe's and Fillmore's) the sequencing of items takes place after 'realization' or 'transformation' rules structurate the sequence-free (deep) semantic structures into syntactic structures. We will now discuss the Fillmorian theory of 'case' in detail. Fillmore's contention has been that since the 'surface' organization of the

---

[1]. Chafe (1970) claimed that nouns identified as 'old' serve as subjects of the sentence. Hence in *John broke his arm, John* is old information as well as the subject of the sentence. Later he changed his stand: "There is no necessary correlation of subject status with givenness, or for that matter of non-subject status with newness." (1976: 48)

sentence and its 'deep' (semantic) structure are assymetrical the grammar should contain a set of syntactic-semantic functions, as well as rules for their realization in their surface structure of a sentence.

Fillmore considers subject and object as surface structure categories, while cases as semantic categories exhibiting the syntactic-semantic relationship between noun(s) and verb(s). He proposes that the deep structure of a sentence consists of **Modality** and a **Proposition**. The former indicates features like negation, tense, mood and aspect. Proposition, according to Fillmore, should consist of a *verb* followed by a sequence of one or more cases. Hence proposition is written as:

P ─────────→ V + (Agent) (Experiencer) (Instrument)
                           (Objective) (Locative)   (Factitive)

Case	*Semantic function*
(1) Agentive (AGT)	Instigator of the action and typically animate identified by the verb.
(2) Experiencer (EXP)	The animate being affected by the state or action, or the animate being which receives or accepts or experiences or undergoes the effect of an action (originally this was dative).
(3) Instrumental (INST)	Inanimate force object causally involved in the action or state identified by the verb, as well as the stimulus or immediate physical cause of an event.
(4) Objective (OBJ)	Object affected by the action or state identified by the verb.
(5) Locative (LOC)	The case that identifies the location or spatial orientation of the state or action identified by the verb.

(6) Factitive (FACT)　　Object or being remitting from the action or state identified by the verb or understood as part of the meaning of the verb.

The following sentences exhibit each of the case relations mentioned above.

1. *John* opened the door (AGT).
2. *John* is sad (EXP).
3. John opened the door *with a key* (INST).
4. The *door* opened (OBJ).
5. *Chicago* is windy (LOC).
6. The carpenters built *the table* (FACT).

Once the case categories were defined as deep structure categories the nouns occupying such cases can appear in any position in the surface structure without disturbing the case relation. Hence in the following pair of sentences *John is* the agent in (7) and (8) but not the subject in (8).

7. John opened the door.
   (John = subject, agent)
8. The door was opened by John.
   (John = agent; door = subject)

The constant, therefore, is the semantic relationship rather than the syntactic role. We add a few more examples to identify other semantic relationships:

9. (a) John gave Jill the doll.
   (b) John gave the doll to Jill.
   (c) Jill was given the doll by John.
   (d) The doll was given to Jill by John.

Again each noun (John, Jill and doll) stand in the same semantic relationship (AGT, EXP and OBJ respectively) regardless of its syntactic position. *John* is always the agent, *Jill* is always the experiencer (or dative) because the noun Jill benefits by the action even though it is grammatically an indirect object in (a) and (d), the object of a preposition in (b), and the subject in (c).

In the later versions (1970-71) Fillmore distinguished between Goal and Source. The former was defined as the end point of the movement of an object in the case of movement verbs and it identifies the final stage into which an object develops into in the case of 'state of change' verbs. For instance:

10. I reached the *university* in half an hour.
11. The tailor made a *beautiful dress* out of an old piece of cloth.

Sentence (11) would be assigned the following deep structure: 11.

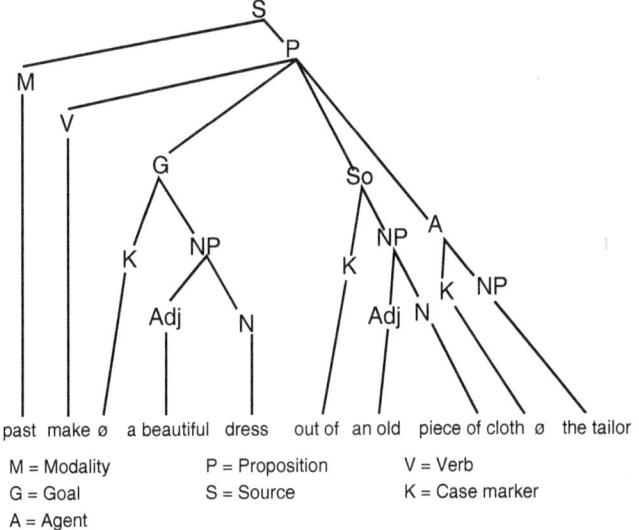

M = Modality   P = Proposition   V = Verb
G = Goal   S = Source   K = Case marker
A = Agent

Source was defined as the starting point of the movement of an object in the case of the movement verbs and is the starting state of the object which undergoes the change of state verbs. *An old piece of cloth* in the above example is the case of Source.

Given this approach, the sentences of a language can be described as consisting of a varying number of nouns, each specified as having a semantically defined case relationship to the verb associated with it. Each case configuration provides a sentence frame into which certain verbs can be inserted and others cannot. For example, the verb *open* can have the following case:

open [——OBJ (AGT) (INST)]

since OBJECTIVE N is obligatory and the other two are optional as can be seen in the following examples:

(a) The door opened (OBJ).
(b) John opened the door (AGT + OBJ).
(c) John opened the door with a key, (AGT + OBJ + INST).

Similarly, the verb *run*, for example, may be inserted into the frame (—A), the verb *sad* into the frame (—E), verbs like *murder* and *terrorize* into (—E A), and so on.

Fillmore proposes that each case frame will give all the syntactic and semantic information about the verb in question. The syntactic information, at times, triggers the appropriate transformation to operate. Thus, Fillmore suggests that "verbs are distinguished from each other not only by specification of the case frames into which they can be inserted but also by their transformational properties" (1971c).

Very specific rules are made to realize the surface structure categories. For example, Fillmore posited the hierarchy AEIOSG to show that the left-most element becomes the subject.

Hence, Fillmorian grammar involved choosing the right verb with maximum and minimum number of cases befitting the appropriate 'case frame' and assigning the subject-object categories only in the surface structure. This helped him relate causative verbs with non-causatives. For instance, in phrases like

12. John opened the door with a key (AGT OBJ INST).
13. The door opened (inchoative) (OBJ).

Fillmore treats the verb *open* in both these sentences as the same verb differentiated only by their different case frames. The same semantic representation is assigned to both these sentences. The difference in meaning is ascribed to the presence or absence of an agent phrase. Morphologically unrelated causative and inchoative such as *kill* and *die* can also be treated in the same way. In this way they can be considered synonymous. Pairs of verbs related as converses such as *like* and *please* in sentences (14) and (15) can be regarded as synonymous with identical case frames differing only with respect to which case must be selected as the subject.

14. The audience *liked* the Prime Minister's lecture.
15. The Prime Minister's lecture *pleased* the audience.

Once each case is so well defined the selectional features of the accompanying noun do not need to be specified obligatorily.[2]

---

2. Though Fillmore does give the obligatory rule of the following type which specifies that any N in an A (gentive) or D (ative) phrase must contain the feature (+ animate)

    N ————— [+ animate] / A,D [X—————Y]

2.5.1 Communication and Presupposition

Fillmore maintains the distinction between the relevant communicative components of the meaning of a word and the presuppositions which ensure a correct choice of the referent, but do not belong to that which is asserted. Of the four components forming the meaning of a word, *bachelor*—(1) human, (2) adult, (3) male, (4) never married—only the last is relevant to the communication, only the fourth feature is subject to negation. Thus in the sentence *Mohan is not a bachelor,* the fact that Mohan is an adult male is not denied. What is denied is that he is not married (see also 3.4.3).

Fillmore has also attracted our attention to words called "connotative predicates" *(even, still, only, also, already,* etc.) which besides transmitting the basic information content of the utterance also explicates the connotative meaning. Thus, the meaning of the sentence *Mohan is even taller than Ram* can be viewed as a conjunction of two propositions: (1) *Mohan is taller than Ram,* and (2) *Ram is tall:* the latter includes a relational concept (tall) and must be read as *Ram is taller than an average man.*

Fillmore's excellent study on the meaning of verbs of judgements has demonstrated that there are languages which have pairs of words which differ in the distribution of their semantic content between presupposition and assertion; e.g. *to accuse* (presupposes negative evaluation of an act) and *to criticize* (assertion of agent's responsibility towards the act) (Fillmore, 1967, 1971c).

To conclude, Fillmore sets up an opposition between the denotative (semantic) principle of sentence description and the logico-communicative principle of lexical description. The deep syntactic structure, according to Fillmore, is universal, and the typological differences between languages are to be found in the manner this deep structure is realized in the surface.

The Fillmorian theory of case grammar can be viewed schematically as:

BASE $\begin{cases} 1. \text{ Case frames and frame features} \\ 2. \text{ Selectional features of nouns} \\ 3. \text{ Other syntactic information} \end{cases}$

$\downarrow$
Transformations
$\downarrow$
Surface structure with subject-object categories

Fig. 3

2.6.0 Chomsky's Views (1957)

His views on the place of meaning in grammar have undergone several changes from the 1957 stand given in *Syntactic Structures* (1957) to, let us say, the 1975 stand taken in *Reflections on Language* and in *Lectures on Government and Binding* (1981) and more recently in his minimalist theory (1986, 1995 and 2000).

2.6.1 Syntactic Structures (1957), Aspects (1965) and EST (1971)

In *Syntactic Structures* Chomsky's main concern was to investigate into the native speaker's ability to distinguish a grammatical sentence from a non-grammatical one. The status of meaning was outside of linguistics proper and "clearly secondary to the description of syntax" (Maclay 1971: 169). During this period Chomsky's explication of meaning was restricted to finding out "the way in which the syntactic structure is put to use in actual functioning of language"

(1957: 102). It had no relevance whatsoever in the construction of a grammar. Here his own words are very interesting and also very amusing: "A great deal of effort has been expended in attempting to answer the question: 'How can you construct a grammar with no appeal to meaning?' The question itself, however, is wrongly put, since the implication that obviously one can construct a grammar *with* appeal to meaning is totally unsupported. One might with equal justification ask: 'How can you construct a grammar with no knowledge of hair colour of speakers?' (1957: 93)."

It was only in 1965 that he distinguished between surface structure and deep structure of a sentence, meaning thereby the number of interpretations a single sentence can have. Chomsky's handling of semantic information in a grammar as described in *Aspects of the Theory of Syntax (1965),* also known as the Standard Theory (ST), is more or less the same as explicated by Fodor and Katz (1963) and Katz and Postal (1964). (See Section 2.2.1 of this book.) In ST the deep structure of a sentence was to be semantically interpreted by the semantic component which in turn was composed of Dictionary and Projection rules. These deep structures were generated by the *base* component of the grammar. Base itself was composed of categorial ruics, lexicon and lexical insertion rules. Hence, a word like *colourful* would have the following information *in* the Base:

[+ Adj]
[+ A NP]   [+ human subject/object]
                [− animate subject/object]

Later the semantic component with the help of the dictionary and projection rules would give the full information regarding the word colourful as follows:

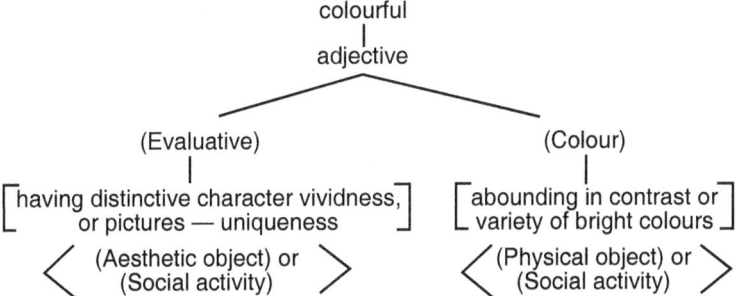

Where markers are enclosed in ( ), distinguishers in [ ] and selection restrictions in < >.

Chomsky (1971) revised his ST on the basis of the work by Jackendoff, Kuroda and Emonds. This came to be known as the Extended Standard Theory (EST). He argues in EST that some aspects of meaning can be accounted for only by reference to certain aspects of the surface structure, thus enabling both deep structure and surface structure to get semantic interpretation from the semantic component. Crucial to his arguments are two semantic notions like *focus* and *presupposition* of a sentence which are regularly correlated with its stress and intonation pattern which are surface structure phenomena.

2.6.2 Revised Extended Standard Theory (1975), Trace Theory, Government and Binding (1981)

Now let us look at Chomsky's views as reflected in *Reflections on Language* (1975). Here he abandons his EST in favour of the Revised Extended Standard Theory (REST). He proposes to drop the term 'deep structure' and instead speaks only of 'initial phrase-marker' and 'surface structure' (p. 82). He suggests that terms like 'basic structure' and 'deep grammar' should be used to refer to non-superficial aspects of surface structures, the rules that generate surface structures, the abstract level of initial phrase-markers, the principles that govern the organization of grammar and relate surface structures to semantic representations, and so on (p. 84). Chomsky makes a very significant remark while discussing the following sentences:

1. The police think who the FBI discovered that Bill shot.
2. The police know who the FBI discovered that Bill shot.

He raises the question whether the deviance of sentence (I) is 'syntactic' or 'semantic' and answers that he is not persuaded that any reasonable criteria exist to establish it (p. 95).

Chomsky further finds it reasonable to postulate that *only* surface structures undergo semantic interpretation, though these 'surface structures' are no longer the same as of the ST, because they retain certain traces of the elements of initial structures which were subsequently deleted. One would be tempted to suggest that he should now rename 'surface structures' as 'global structures'. Hence the principal innovation of REST had been the *Trace Theory* meaning thereby a movement rule deposits a trace to keep track of syntactic information that would otherwise be lost in the application of the rule in EST. Chomsky's discussion of the difference in the meaning range of passives and actives (1975: 97-98) is revealing in two ways. It brings out the structural difference between the two. Secondly, and more importantly, it speaks of certain factual judgements and 'connotative' meaning. He notes that two kinds of "grammatical relation" seem to be involved in the interpretation of sentences such as (3) and (4):

3. Beavers build dams.
4. Dams are built by beavers.

One, the relation of verb-object of the initial phrase-marker, accounting for the similarity in meaning between these sentences; and another relation, subject-predicate. of the surface structure, accounting for a difference in meaning.

> *Beavers build dams* is true, but does not imply that all *beavers build dams,* only that beavers are dam-builders: dam-building is a characteristic of the species. But *dams are built by beavers is,* I think, naturally understood to imply that all dams are built by beavers, and is thus false. (1977: 39).

To sum up, let us look at Chomsky's view of the general structure of grammar as explicated in those days. The rules of the categorical component and the lexicon, *i.e.* the base (B), provide initial phrase-markers (IPM). Applying transformations (T) to these, we derive surface structures (SS) *(including traces),* which undergo semantic interpretation (SR-1). The rules of semantic interpretation assign the scope of logical operators ('not', 'each', 'who', etc.) and fix their meaning, assign antecedents to such anaphoric expressions as reciprocals ('each other') and necessarily bound anaphors:

5. John lost *his* way (bound anaphor).
6. John found *his* book (unbound anaphor).

The application of these rules result in 'logical form' (LF). 'Sentence grammar' may come to close at this point.

Sentence grammar: $\xrightarrow{B}$ IPM $\xrightarrow{T}$ SS $\xrightarrow{SR\text{-}1}$ SR-1

Then, to place grammar within the system of cognitive structures generally, he further adds:

> the logical forms so generated are subject to further interpretation by other semantic rules (SR-2) interacting with other cognitive structures, giving fuller representations of meaning.

(SR-2
other systems)   :   LF⟶ 'meaning'

(1975: 104-5)

The SR-2 and 'other systems' may involve discourse properties interacting with considerations of situation, intention and the like.

Chomsky's views of 1975 and 1977 get full formalization in his *Lectures on Government and Binding* (LGB) (1981; see also Chomsky, 1983). Here he proposes the theory of Universal Grammar (UG). The syntactic component of such a grammar generates an infinite set of abstract structures called 'S-structures' that are assigned representations in phonetic forms (PF) and in logical forms (LF). It is to be noted that the mapping of S-structure to PF and LF are independent of one another.

```
           Syntax
             |
         S-structure
          /      \
        PF        LF
```

It is to be noted here that the central concept throughout is 'grammar' not 'language'. The latter is derivative at a higher level of abstraction from actual neural mechanisms.

UG consists of interacting subsystems, which can be considered from various points of view. From our point of view, these are the various sub-components of the rule system of grammars. From another point of view, which has become increasingly important in recent years, is the subsystems of principles. Chomsky assumes that the sub-components of the rule system are the following:

(i) Lexicon

(ii) Syntax
    (a) Categorial component
    (b) Transformational component
(iii) PF component
(iv) LF component.

The subsystem of principles includes the following:

(i) Bounding theory
(ii) Government theory
(iii) θ-theory
(iv) Binding theory
(v) Case theory
(vi) Control theory.

Bounding theory poses locality conditions on certain processes and related items. The central notion of government theory is the relation between the head of a construction and categories dependent on it. θ-theory is concerned with the assignment of thematic roles such as agent of action, etc. (called θ - roles). Binding theory is concerned with relation of anaphors, pronouns, names, and variables to possible antecedents. Case theory deals with assignment of abstract case and its morphological realization. Control theory determines the potential for reference of the abstract pronominal element PRO. After having mentioned all these, Chomsky finds it reasonable to suppose that UG determines a set of core grammars and that what is actually represented in the mind of an individual even under the idealization to a homogeneous speech community would be a core grammar with a periphery of marked elements and constructions (cf. Sadighi, F. and Bavali, M., 2008).

Lectures on Government and Binding should be viewed as one further step in the development of a modular theory that began with Chomsky, 1977, or before. What is important about LGB is that it is the first presentation within a single work of a more or less completely sketched 'example' of a modular theory. It is interesting to note that 'Filters and Control', an early (and even briefer) effort to sketch a complete theory is now almost completely eliminated. Katz (1980) had been very critical of Chomsky for excluding meaning from the grammatical structure of sentences:

> Chomsky's new concept of grammar sacrifices even the possibility of explaining the class of ambiguities that depend on syntactic derivation. (1980: 18).

2.7.0 Shaumyan's Theory (1977)

He rightly says, "the goal of a semantic theory of natural language is to explain the process of linguistic communication, which consists of an exchange of messages by a speaker and a hearer" (1977: vii). To account for such phenomena as ambiguity, paraphrasal relationship, he assumes that each natural language can be split into two languages:

(a) *a primitive language* in which the content of the message is represented unambiguously;

(b) an *expression language* into which the expressions of the primitive language are mapped.

Here expression language means "a language possessing various means for the expression of one and the same language" (p. vii). The universal semiotic system that models semantic process, that is, mappings from natural expression languages is called the genotype language which is connected with the phenotype language, *i.e.* natural language, by correspondence rules which constitute the phenotype grammar.

2.7.1 Genotype and Phenotype Grammars

To Shaumyan, the semantic theory is a formal system in which the following are postulated (p. 56):
1. Sentences of the primitive sub-language of the relator genotype language, which are called *semantic axioms*.
2. A finite set of rules for semantic derivations. Semantic derivations are processes that specify which linguistic forms of sentences correspond to which linguistic meanings of sentences. A set of semantic derivations is obtained from one semantic axiom since one and the same meaning can be embodied in a set of linguistic forms, or, to put it in another way, one situation can have a set of names (p. 57). When two given sentences are mutually substitutable in the process of communication they are considered semantically equivalent (p. 58). A sentence can be described in terms of 'situation' (signifié) and 'expression' (signifiant). A grammar is a set of rules that map the infinite set of unilateral units—situations—into an infinite set of bilateral units—sentences. A grammar can be thought of as a special operator that maps situations onto sentences and sentences onto situations (p. 114).

Shaumyan considers the following as the essential details of what might be called the theory of Constructing Phenotype Grammars (p. 116).
1. Three levels of representation have to be distinguished for situations:
    (i) the content plane (semantic level),
    (ii) the expression plane (phonological level),
    (iii) the level on which (i) and (ii) meet (morphological level): Each level must be split into two sub-levels: deep level and surface level.

2. A grammar must have three components that operate in a sequence:
   (i) a semantic component,
   (ii) a morphological component,
   (iii) a phonological component.

The semantic component operates with unilateral units of meaning called phenotype semions and constructs the deep semantic level, which is mapped onto the surface-semantic level of representation. The morphological component projects the surface-semantic level onto the phonological one, and in the process creates bilateral units called sentences consisting of a signifié and a significant. The phonological component projects the phonological level of representation onto the phonetic one.

3. (i) The deep-semantic level of representation must be constructed as a projection of the primitive sub-language of the relator genotype language.
   (ii) The rules that map the primitive sub-language of the relator genotype language into the expression sub-language of the relator genotype language must also apply in the phenotype grammar to project 'deep situation' onto the 'surface situation'.

Two sorts of rules are involved in the transformation of deep situations into surface ones: (1) genotype semantic rules, and (2) special phenotype semantic rules (p. 117).

4. The operator-operand relation must be kept as the basis for the description of phenotype language (as in the case of genotype language).

5. When a deep situation is projected onto a phonological representation, the meaning of the situation must remain constant.

6. Phonological oppositions cannot be neutralized on the level of the phonological representation.

The above conditions govern the construction of Applicational Grammar of natural languages as conceived by Shaumyan.

2.7.2 Preference Semantics

Wilks (1975) has given us in his Preference Semantics a set of semantic primitives. Preference semantics has access to the senses of words coded as lexical decomposition trees, formed from a finite inventory of semantic primitives. For each phrase or clause of a complex sentence, the system builds up a network of such trees with the aid of structured items called templates (p. 329). These templates are bound together by paraplates and common sense inferences. These three items consist of formulae which in turn consist of elements. Elements are sixty primitive semantic units used to express the semantic entities, states, qualities, actions about which 'humans' speak and write. The elements fall into five classes (p. 331):

(a) *entities* MAN (human beings)
STUFF (substances)
THING (physical object)
PART (parts of things)
FOLK (human groups)
ACT (acts)
STATE (state of existence)
BEAST (animals) etc.

(b) *actions* FORCE (compels)
CAUSE (causes to happen)
FLOW (moving as liquids do)
PICK (choosing)
BE (exists) etc.

(c) *type indicators* KIND (being a quality)
HOW (being a type of action) etc.

(d) *sorts* CONT (being a container)
GOOD (being morally acceptable)
THRU (being an aperture) etc.

(e) *cases* TO (direction)
SOURCE (source)
GOAL (goal or end)
LOCA (location)
SUBJ (actor or agent)
OBJE (patient of action)
IN (containment)
POSS (possessed by) etc.

Formulae are constructed from elements and right and left brackets. The formulae are binarily bracketed lists of whatever depth is necessary to express the word sense. *Drink* is formulated as follows:

((*ANI SUBJ) (((FLOW STUFF) OBJE) (*ANI IN) (((THIS (*ANI (THRU PART))). TO (MOVE CAUSE)))))

This will be interpreted as:

> an action, preferably done by animate things (*ANI SUBJ) to liquids ((FLOW STUFF) OBJE) of causing the liquid to move into the animate thing (*ANI IN) and *via* (TO indicating the direction case) a particular aperture of the animate thing; the mouth of course (p. 332).

A template consists of a network of formulae grounded on a basic actor–action–object triple of formulae, e.g. small men sometimes father big sons.

(1) KIND MAN HOW MAN KIND MAN.
(2) KIND MAN HOW CAUSE KIND MAN.

(CAUSE is the head of the verbal sense *of father, to father* has to be analysed *as to cause to have life.*)

It has rightly been emphasized by Wilks that the template is the sequence of formulae, and not to be confused with the triple of elements (heads) used to locate it (p. 333). He also says that his system directs itself, at each stage, towards the correct network by always opting for the most 'semantically dense' one it can construct (p. 329). He adds that the notion of preferring a semantic network with the greatest possible semantic density is a natural way of dealing not only with normal semantic disambiguation but also with metaphor (p. 342).

2.8.0 Pragmatics

Pragmatics can be understood if it is placed in the context of two more terms which together constitute the trinity of semiotics. *Semiotics* is the study of sign-systems. *Syntactics* studies the relations holding among signs. *Semantics* studies the relations between signs and their referents. *Pragmatics* studies the relations between signs and their human users. Pragmatics can also be considered as the study of linguistic indices, and indices can be interpreted only when they are used. In other words pragmatics is the study of meaning at the level of a given context. The study of pragmatics presented here is mainly based on Bates (1976).

2.8.1 Performatives, Presuppositions and Conversational Postulates

Performatives describe the intention of the speaker to use a sentence as a question, a command, etc. This aspect is covered under the Interpersonal function of Systemic Functional Grammar (see section 3.4.1). *Presuppositions* are assumptions about the context that are necessary to make that sentence verifiable, appropriate, or both. *Conversational postulates* are a particular class of presuppositions about the nature of human dialogue in general. Presupposition is said to be of three varieties: semantic, pragmatic and psychological. Bates's analysis is very useful in this regard. Let us look at the following examples:

(a) Mohan has a brother.
(b) Mohan has a male sibling.
(c) Mohan's parents had more than one child.
(d) Mohan exists.

Very different relationships exist among these sentences (propositions):

1. If a is true, b is true too.
   If a is false, b is false too.
   the relationship between (a) and (b) is one of *assertion*.
2. If a is true, c is true too.
   If a is false, no conclusion could be drawn regarding c.
   the relationship between (a) and (c) is one of *entailment*.
3. If a is true, d is true too.
   (even) If a is false, d is true.
   the relationship between (a) and (d) is one of
   presupposition.

Any information implied by a sentence, which is not affected by the negation of that sentence, is a presupposition. The presupposition discussed above is semantic presupposition. Pragmatic presuppositions are concerned with the relationship between a sentence and the context in which it is used. They vary according to the context and the beliefs of the interlocutors. For example the condition 'adult male' is semantically entailed by sentence "Mohan is a bachelor". It is a pragmatic presupposition, necessary for the following sentences to be appropriate:

1. Mohan is a bachelor.
2. Mohan is not a bachelor.

A presupposition can be psychologically present regardless of its overt manifestation, as long as both the speaker and the listener share the *act* of presupposing, or as long as the speaker *thinks* that the act is shared. This type of presupposition is a cognitive activity of relating sentences to contexts which is taken care of by the textual function of Systemic Functional Grammar.

Vennemann (1975) has very illuminating remarks to make regarding presuppositions. He says that they are carried in a special 'presupposition pool' which does not belong to individual sentences, but to entire discourses or, at least, stretches of discourses. The information contained in this pool is constituted (i) from general knowledge, (ii) from the situative context of the discourse, and (iii) from the completed part of the discourse itself. Each participant of a discourse is operating with his own presupposition pool, which grows as the discourse proceeds (see also Section 3.4.2).

Here we can refer to the difference Strawson makes between Reference and Meaning:

> *Reference:* the use of a word or phrase by a speaker to stand for an entity/event in the outside world, or an entity/event in his own imagined world.
>
> *Meaning:* the set of mental acts or operations that a speaker intends to create in his listener by using a sentence.

2.8.2 Proposition

It is more an internal activity of speakers rather than an object located in sentences. Proposition is a *state* or *change* predicated of one argument, or a *relationship* predicated of two or more arguments. When a proposition gets used by a speaker with a specific goal it becomes a speech act. Speech acts are of three types: (1) **Locutions**, (2) **Illocutions**, and (3) **Perlocutions**.

Locutions are required for the making of speech, constructing propositions, and uttering sounds:

   3. He said to me "go away".

Illocutions are the conventional social acts of ordering, abusing, urging etc.:

   4. He urged me to go away.

Perlocutions create the effects planned or emplanned of having used a sentence:

   5. He persuaded me to go away.

The illocutionary act is signalled by a series of elements: intonation, the mood of the verb, the presence of an explicit performative verb. In written language it is signalled by punctuation and in spoken language by extralinguistic context. Leaving the details of structural representation aside, it is imperative to accept that 'performatives' appear somewhere in the psychological make-up of speakers as the speaker's goal in using a sentence. We can view performatives as intentions (cf. Sanskrit *vivaksha* and *tātparya*) that belong to the speaker with respect to his sentence.

2.8.3 Opacity

Cole (1978) proposes that *opacity* results when a sentence containing an attributive description is embedded beneath a verb of propositional attitude or, alternatively, when a proposition contains a description used attributively within the scope of a predicate of propositional attitude. He discusses the following sentence to illustrate his point:

6. Tom believes that the *best doctor* spares no effort to save a patient.

The opaque interpretation (6') is generic and attributive and the transparent interpretation (6") is specific and referential.

(6')

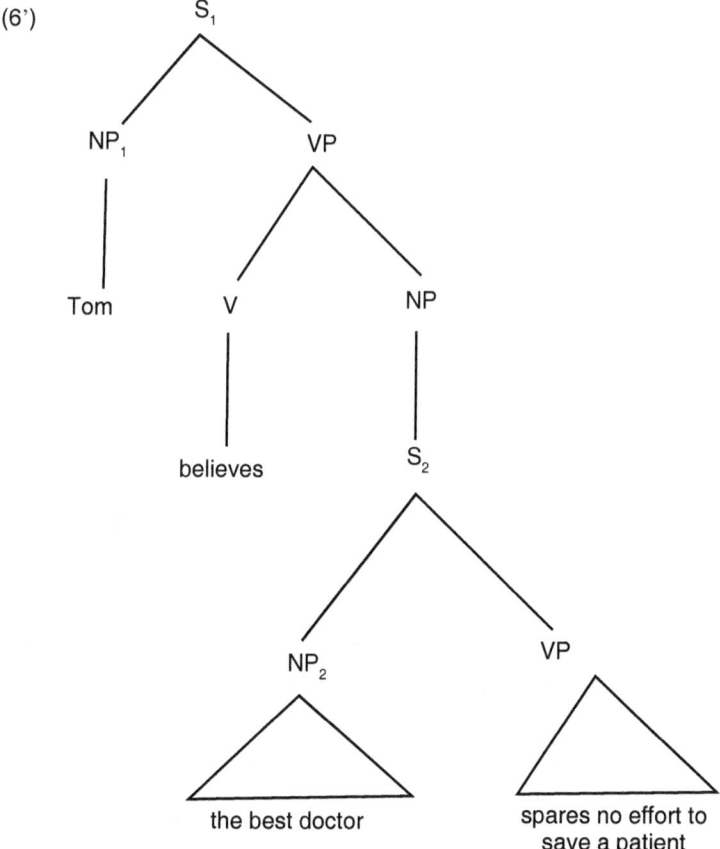

(6'')

```
                    S₀
                   / \
                NP₂   S₁
               /|\   / \
        the best doctor NP₁ VP
                      |  / \
                     Tom V   NP
                         |    |
                     believes S₂
                              / \
                            NP₂  VP
                             |   /|\
                             he spares no effort to
                                save a patient
```

2.8.4 Negation

It is very interesting to note that we cannot negate a lexical item of negative quality (e.g. Solomon was *not a bad king*) unless the context somehow presupposes the statement of negative quality. This restriction does not seem to exist in the case of a positive item (e.g. Solomon was not a *good* king). Here too of course 'good' has to be presupposed as a general requirement. On the other hand 'bad' has to be more specifically presupposed. As such, negatives are more marked in terms of presupposition. Talmy Givon (1978) rightly says that negatives are uttered in a context where corresponding affirmatives have already been discussed, or else where the speaker assumes the hearer's belief in, and thus familiarity with, the corresponding affirmative (p. 109).

2.8.5 Implicatures

We shall wind up our discussion of pragmatics with a note on *implicatures*. Besides knowledge of the conventions of word meanings and the semantic rules of combination, language users also have knowledge about the use of particular expressions or classes of expressions. The conventions of usage take care of occasion, purpose and means (Morgan 1978: 269). Grice says that for a large class of utterances, the total signification of an utterance may be regarded as divisible in two different ways:

(i) What is 'said' and what is 'implicated'.
(ii) What is 'conventionally implicated' and what is 'non-conventionally implicated' (Grice, 1978: 113).

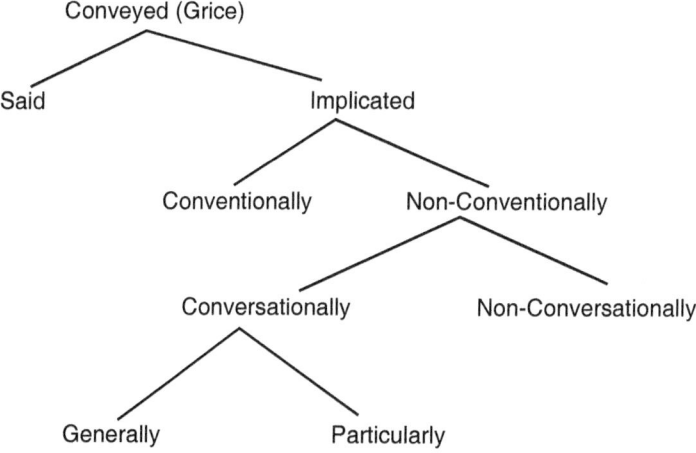

Morgan explains these distinctions quite thoroughly (1978: 282). Conventional implicatures are non-truth conditional aspects of what is conveyed by an utterance solely due to the words or forms the sentence contains. These include the presuppositions of a sentence. Conversational implicatures are derived from the content of the sentences used and owe their existence to the fact that participants in a conversation are constrained by the common goal of communication to be cooperative. The particularized conversational implicatures are crucially dependent not only on the content of the utterance but also on the context of the utterance. The generalized conversational implicatures are relatively independent of context: Saddock's (1974) picturization is slightly different from Grice's (ibid: 284):

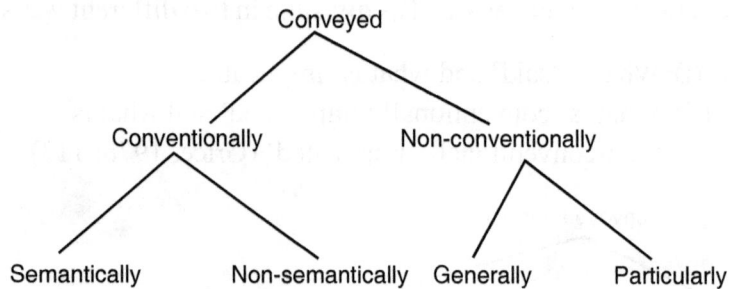

CHAPTER III
The Contextual and Functional View of Meaning

3.1.0 Firth and Malinowski

In this chapter we would like to discuss in detail the theory of meaning that can be attributed to Firth and Halliday. Firth's ideas on meaning (seem to) have been largely influenced by Malinowski's ideas and the ancient Indian theories of meaning. Firth says that the complete meaning of a word is always contextual, and no study of meaning independent of a complete context can be taken seriously. He adds that each word when used in a new context is a new word. He emphasizes that *the disciplines and techniques of linguistics are directed to assist us in making statements of meaning.*

3.1.1 Meaning and Contextual Relations

Firth says that meaning has to be regarded as a complex of contextual relations, and phonetics, grammar, lexicography and semantics each handles its own components of the complex in its appropriate context (see Firth, 1957: 19-26). Meaning is a cover term to account for the following functions:

1. Phonetic function
2. Lexical function
3. Morphological function
4. Syntactic function
5. Context of situation (semantic function).

According to Firth we establish ourselves on speaking terms with our environment, and our words serve our familiarity with it. "The study of words in cultural familiarity" describes the semantic aspect of language (p. 29). This theme is recurrent in Firthian writings. "To begin with, we must apprehend language events in their contexts as shaped by the creative acts of speaking persons" (p. 193). There is an association of social and personal attitude in recurrent contexts of situation with certain phonological features (p. 194) (see Halliday, 1967a, Brazil, 1975, Prakasam, 1979).

Collocation is an important concept of the Firthian theory of semantics. Meaning by *collocation* is an abstraction at the syntagmatic level and is not directly concerned with the conceptual or idea approach to meanings of words (Firth, 1957: 196). The collocations can be *normal* or *unique* and *personal* or *anormal*. Firth uses the expression 'lower modes of meaning' to refer chiefly to the handling of meaning at the phonetic, phonological, prosodic and grammatical levels of abstraction (p. 198). He proposes the following as the categories of the context of situation (p. 203):

A. The relevant features of participants: persons and personalities:

(i) the verbal action of the participants,

(ii) the non-verbal action of the participants.

B. The relevant objects.

C. The effects of verbal action.

Firth's ideas presented above have been adopted and well developed by Halliday, Ellis, Dixon and several other linguists. We shall present here their ideas in a comprehensive framework with adequate modifications wherever found necessary. For the sake of convenience, let us postulate the following different levels and interlevels at which we can analyse a language and account for its features and properties.

Linguistic Sciences					
Phonetics		Linguistics	Semantics	
Substance	Medium	Form	Context	Situation
Phonic or Graphic	Phonology or Graphology	Grammar	Semantic content	Cognitive (psycho-physical)
		Lexis	Pragmatic content	Environ-mental (Socio-cultural)
Language Variation				Institutional

Fig. 1: Levels of Linguistic Analysis

3.1.2 Levels of Meaning

In our account of language, meaning is perceived at the level of 'Form' and the interlevels of 'medium' and 'context'. The medium of a given text can be either graphological or phonological. Meaning at this interlevel we shall call *significance*, which means 'phonological or graphological meaning'. Under the level of Form, we have two demilevels—grammar and lexis. The break in the dividing lines of grammar and lexis, and semantics and pragmatics is indicative of the clinal relationship between the members of each set. In other words one cannot make an absolute distinction between lexis and grammar and between semantics and pragmatics. The meaning we find within grammar and lexis we shall call *Value*. And finally meaning at the interlevel of context we shall call *Content*. Here, then, we have the following types of meaning:

1. Phonological significance (or) graphological significance
2. (a) Grammatical value
   (b) Lexical value

3. (a) Semantic content
   (b) Pragmatic content.

The interlevel of context establishes relationship between the situational features and the formal items or categories (lexicogrammatical items). The situational features may be said to be of three types.

(i) the cognitive (psychophysical)
(ii) the environmental (sociological)
(iii) the institutional.

The *cognitive level* (sub- or demi-level) gives us information about the speaker's (and the hearer's) conceptualization of the real world phenomena (participants, processes, circumstantials, logical relations, informational and discoursal features).

The *environmental level* is related to the cultural representation of the world phenomena. It includes a given speaker's attitude, temperament, mood and the like and the presence of the physical objects at the time of speech act. The cognitive level material gets reflected to a large extent in the semantic layer of the contextual interlevel. The environmental level material gets reflected in the pragmatic layer of the contextual interlevel. Semantic and pragmatic layers are like Siamese twins. One is tempted to agree with George Lakoff that pragmatics and semantics are inseparable (1973). Hence the link in the Fig. 1 shown by way of a break in the dividing line.

The *institutional level* is a paralinguistic or extra-linguistic level which accounts for language variation at the interlevels and the level of Form. It takes care of distinctions like dialect, sociolect, register, and style. Any formally (lexicogrammatically) *valuable* construction will yield *acceptable content* when it is studied with reference to all these features, though certain sentences might demand a lot of imagination to find them a pragmatic and thence semantic placement.

When we talk of these levels we can also make more delicate statements (of superordinate-subordinate nature). The situation (i) could be *immediate* (x) or *wider* (y). The immediate congnitive situation will give us 'thesis' (Ellis, 1966: 84). By thesis is meant the event, process, action, state of affairs, etc., to which a given utterance refers. Ellis rightly calls it as the component creating 'a secondary universe' (1 x) to the 'primary universe' (1 y). The thesis of the utterance "(he is) running" can be said to be one of the existence and realization of the concept of 'swift movement'—this analysis is at a particular point on the scale of delicacy (see Halliday, 1961, in Kress, 1975) which means one can get at more delicate descriptions of this movement. The wider situation, that is, the 'universe' of the given utterance involves broader concepts like 'movement' and 'non-movement'.

The environmental (sociological) level too yields several subclasses on the immediate (x) and wider (y) dimensions. The other dimensions that are important are given the following labels: (a) topic, (b) personalities. With these dimensions, we will get the following features.

2 xa : xy motive   2 xb : xy roles
2 ya : xy motif   2 yb : xy participants.

The 'motif' of an utterance like "how do you do" is one of *maintaining certain courtesies* and the 'motive' is one of 'greeting at the time of first meeting'. In an expression like "How are we feeling today Mrs. James", the motif is enquiry and the motive is 'the enquiry which is *personal*', that too about the addressee herself as contrasted with "How is your husband today, Mrs. James" (Ellis, 1966). Incidentally, the thesis of both the statements is one of 'health' and the 'universe' involves concepts of health, ill health, well-being and the like. In the first sentence the personalities in wider situation (i.e., participants) are *doctor* or *nurse and patient* and in immediate situation (i.e. roles) are *speaker* (or 'wisher') and *hearer* ('wished'). An intermediate point can be postulated on this scale of 'immediate' and 'wide'points where, in 'this case, we can have the 'performer' and the 'non-performer'. Participants 'are 'acteur' and 'roles' are 'actant' in Greimas's actantial model.

The features of the 'institutional' built on the dimensions of dialect (a), sociolect (b), register (c), style (d) are as follows:

3 xa : dialect-choice; 3 ya : dialect-range.
3 xb : sociolect-choice, 3 yb : sociolect-range.
3 xc : register-choice; 3 yc : register-range.
3 xd : style-choice,   3 yd : style-range.

Dialect is a language variety on the dimension of 'local' origin of the performer. *Sociolect is a* language variety on the dimension 'statuscum-social' origin of the performer. *Register* is the language variety identified on the dimensions of (i) *field*—subject matter (province of reference), and (ii) *role*—conversation, literacy, etc. *Style is* a language variety identified on the dimensions of (i) 'formality' (e.g. formal, casual intimate, frozen, consultative), and (ii) *mode* (e.g. written, tape-recorded, broadcast, etc).

By dialect-range is meant the total repertory of dialects of the performer, his idiolect classified from a dialect point of view. By dialect-choice is meant the particular dialect out of the performer's range to which the utterance may be assigned. The distinction of 'range' and 'choice' operates on the same lines with other language varieties too. The discussion we have had above yields the Table 1.

3.2.1 Significance

Let's now get into different types of meaning in greater detail. As we have stated above, the *phonological* or *graphological* meaning will be labelled *significance*. We can recognize three types of features in phonology/graphology: '-ematic', '-sodic' and '-ational'. The alternate levels (not demi-levels) yield us three features each: (See Table 2).

Table 1: The Level of Situation

Demi-levels	Immediate (x)	Wider (y)		
Cognitive	thesis	universe		
Environmental	motive	motif	topic (a)	
	role	participant	personalities (b)	
Institutional	dialect choice	dialect-range	dialect (a)	
	sociolect-choice	sociolect-range	sociolect (b)	
	register-choice	register-range	register (c)	
	style-choice	style-range	style (d)	

All the above are situational categories which help us arrive at the 'content' of well-formed chunks of utterance with certain 'values' of their own.

Table 2: The Interlevel of Medium

	Phonology	Graphology
'-ematic	phonematic units	Graphematic units
'-sodic	prosodic features	Grosodic features
'-ational	Intonational features	Graphational features

Phonematic units (or phonegments) are those which are abstracted as minimal units by analysing the speech sounds of a given language. Graphematic units are those which are used in writing. '-ematic' units are those which have unisegmental value.

Graphematic units	Phonematic units
i	/i/
e	/e/
a	/æ/
	/a/
	/o/

Here we have avoided the more abstract practice of separating syntagmatic features from their paradigmatic associates (cf. discussion in Prakasam, 1981).

Prosodic features are those supersegmental (non-unisegmental) features which go with the syllables and feet of the phonological hierarchy.

'Stress' in English and 'tone' in Punjabi are prosodic features. We have separated the intonational features from prosodic features for several reasons. Neither phonematic units nor prosodic features expound content distinctions. But the intonational features help us distinguish between different types of utterance especially with reference to attitudes and 'mood' (question, statement), the phonematic and prosodic elements remaining the same. Some prosodic features get represented in certain scripts and such features can be called 'grosodic features'. The punctuation marks like /./,/ 1,/ &/;/ are 'graphational' features because they are intended to reflect in writing intonational features. However it needs to be noted that all the graphational features current in a writing system may not reflect intonational features. If a writing system is revised so as to bring in good equation between the two sets of features it would be quite profitable.

The 'significance' of a language involves a systematic study of the phonematic units, the prosodic and the intonational features. The meaning of a phonematic unit is the consideration of its syntagmatic and paradigmatic possibilities. For example, in English the significance of [ŋ] involves a study which leads to statements of the following type:

  (i) it cannot occur initially
 (ii) it occurs finally or before /k/ and /g/
(iii) it contrasts with non-nasal velars: /k/ and /g/
 (iv) it contrasts with non-velar nasals: /m/ and /n/.

To quote Ellis: "the phonological (graphological) meanning of an item such as a term in a phonological system is its relation to other phonological items, its place in the total phonological system concerned" (1966: 80). Often we come across statements like "the contrast of presence of aspiration and its absence is meaningless in English". Such a distinction will be proved invalid when a phonetic description is given to an 'instance' of the phonematic unit in an utterance, and a prosodic feature will be imposed on the phonematic unit in such instantial description. The absence or presence of aspiration will be indicative of the phonic environment or the nonnative background of the speaker. In either case aspiration is 'significant'. Here 'significant' means much more than 'meaning-changing' ability.

3.2.2 Value

Let's now move over to 'value', the meaning of grammatical categories. To quote Ellis again: "The formal meaning of a formal item or category, either grammatical or lexical, is its relation to other formal items or categories. Phonological and formal meaning correspond to the information of 'information theory' in being dependent on, and questionable in terms of, the number of oppositions in a given system" (1966: 80). Dixon says that formal meaning is "the meaning of a piece of language with respect to its internal patternings" (1964: 23). He further says: "Two items will be said to have different formal meanings if and only if they receive distinct descriptions in terms of the categories of grammar and lexis for the language to which they belong." To discuss the value of 'a grammatical unit' or 'a lexical item' we shall have to consider each on two axes—the *syntagmatic* and *the paradigmatic*.

On the syntagmatic axis, a grammatical unit (e.g. sentence, clause, group, word, morpheme) has certain colligational privileges i.e. it has certain 'patterns' and structural possibilities. For example in English clause 'goal' or 'actor' can be 'subject' whereas 'attribute' or 'range' cannot be. An item in a 'system' will have one kind of value when it colligates with a particular item from another system and the value changes when it colligates with a different item. The value of a clause will be one when it has a goal complement and it will be different when it has a range complement. In the first case the clause of that structure will have a 'receptive' counterpart (or 'allosentence or 'agnate clause' (Verma, 1968-69, Halliday, 1967b)), whereas the second one cannot:

(i) (a) He walked a horse (operative).
     (b) A horse was walked by him (receptive).
(ii) (a) He walked ten miles.
  *(b) Ten miles was walked by him.

The value of 'walk' is different in these clauses. It is determined by its place in the system of verbal group. This consideration is on paradigmatic axis. A 'system' is a closed set of features which are distinct from one another. An item from the system enters into a particular structure. This is a colligational restriction. For example, a passive verbal group cannot be followed by a 'complement/actor' but can be by an 'adjunct/actor'.

sub/goal	passive predication /process	adjunct/actor
(iii) The song	was sung	by John
sub	predicator	comp
*(iv) the song	was sung	John

The second utterance will be acceptable if 'John' is "complement/beneficiary".

A lexical item is "a formal item (at least one morpheme) whose pattern of occurrence can be described in terms of uniquely ordered series of other lexical items occurring in its environments" (Sinclair, 1966: 142). A lexical item will have a 'scatter'. For example, the item 'strong' has the following scatter: *strong, strongly, strength, strengthen, stronger, strongest.* It has on the chain the possibility of co-occurring with items like 'argument' and 'tea', and has partial choice relationship with 'powerful':

strong argument strong tea
powerful argument *powerful tea

3.3.1 Lexis

We will now note here three important observations of Halliday regarding lexis (1966: 152-58):

1. Lexis seems to require the recognition merely of linear co-occurrence together with some measure of singificant proximity, either a scale or at least a cut off point. It is this syntagmatic relation which is referred to as 'collocation'.... In the place of grammatical closed system, lexis requires open-ended 'set' assignment which is

best regarded probabilistic. Collocation and lexical set are mutually defining as are structure and system. The set is the grouping of members with like privilege of occurrence in collocation.
2. In grammar, a 'bridge' category is required between the element of structure and the term in the system on the one hand and the formal item on the other and this is the class. But in lexis the item is directly referable to the categories of collocation and set.
3. The lexical item is not necessarily coextensive on either axis with the item, or rather with any of the items, identified and accounted for in the 'grammar'. So it may be useful to recognize, on the syntagmatic axis, a lexical item which has defined status in the grammar and is not identified as morpheme, word, or group, e.g. 'let in for', 'come out with'. Viewed from this angle a lexical item can be *simple, compound* or *phrasal.*

The meaning of a lexical item (value) will be a statement on the following parameters:

1. type of the lexical item: simple, compound, phrasal
2. scatter
3. collocational span or range
4. lexical set.

All formal patterns have certain 'value' as they enter into 'patterns' and 'systems' grammatically and 'ranges' and 'sets' lexically. A statement of 'value' of a formal item will consist in the discussion of its 'grammatical' and 'lexical' properties, possibilities of co-occurrence and its restrictions, and of substitutability and its restrictions. Once we know the 'significance' and 'value' of a piece of language, we will be

Chapter 3 ▮ The Contextual and Functional View of Meaning

ready to discuss its 'content' at the interlevel of context by relating it to the relevant features of situation. However it needs to be noted that we can get at the 'significance' and 'value' of the forms of a language only after observing their behaviour in actual speech situations. So the process is recursive and bidirectional.

The contextual meaning of a piece of language is its meaning with respect to the correspondence that can be set up between its internal patterns and the relevant patterns in its general situation (cf. Dixon, 1964). Ellis rightly says that we can formulate 'content' as a network of relations within context, systemic and structural ones of the 'value' type. All formal items, both grammatical items and lexical items, have contextual meaning (Ellis, 1966: 80-81). The situational features which we have noted above are 'universal' categories. What differs for different languages is the selection of situational features made by the different systems of contextual meaning. Our 'situation' is the same as Hjelmslev's 'content substance' and our 'context' is similar to his 'content form'. Content is either potential or instantial (actual). The potential content of a formal item is the range of possible contents of that item considered in abstraction from any text. Its instantial content is the actual content in a given instance of occurrence in a given place in a given text with a given situation. Ellis postulates between two extremes a line of 'potentiality/ instantiality', and associated with it is the *scale of delicacy of focus* (p. 87). He says that the utterance (instantial meaning) is the unit of form related to situation. On the basis of utterance and the formal categories of a given language we can abstract the categories of the context of the given language (potential meaning). The unit of form related to context is the potential utterance, and here the minimal unit is the sentence. Here one can refer to Antal's viewpoint: "The sentence is the minimum unit of content and at the same time the maximum unit of the meaning." Antal's 'meaning' (see also Section 1.1.10) is similar to our 'value'. He says that 'meaning' unites the form of the sentence (its signs) and the content of the sentence and that it explains the observable regularity in the use of signs (33-37).

3.3.2 Potentiality and Instantiality

The scale of potentiality and instantiality is also associated with the scale of 'notion'. The more delicate the notion is, the nearer we are to the 'instantial' meaning. The delicacy of focus is the relation between contextual meaning and thesis or between contextual meanings (Ellis, 1966: 86-87).

The situational relation $t\theta < ts$ (= a lesser time than before) yields the contextual meaning $tR =$ past ($R =$ reference, potential contextual meaning corresponding to thesis).

$t\theta < ts$: $tr =$ Past
$t\theta \supset ts$: $tR =$ Future
$t\theta = ts$: $tR =$ Present (i.e. not exclusively past or future)

where $=$ is a relation other than exclusively before or after, including $\supset$ (includes) and $<>$ (before and after). ($t\theta =$ time of thesis; $ts =$ time of speech; $tR =$ tense representation. Ellis describes the 'tense' aspect of the utterance.

> They'll have been going to have been building a National theatre for ten years now.

as follows (1966: 89):

$t\theta_1 > ts, t\theta_2 < t\theta_1, t\theta_3 > t\theta_2, t\theta_4 < t\theta_3, t\theta_5 \supset t\theta_4,$.

Dixon generalizes that the elements from successive matrices associated with successive processes of language in a text will

Chapter 3 ■ *The Contextual and Functional View of Meaning* 91

correspond to contextual descriptions which are consistent with one another and in which a chain of continuity can be recognized (1964: 40). Ambiguity cannot be present if the 'value' of a formal item and its 'situation' were allowed to be scientifically relevant to its linguistic consideration. A given chunk of utterance will be assigned its content if we are given the 'wider' and 'immediate' features of the situation in which the piece was uttered.

3.3.3 Summary

(i) 'Meaning' has to be discovered at different levels and interlevels of linguistic analysis.
(ii) At each level or interlevel we have to analyse an utterance in terms of *units* and *features* and account for its properties of co-occurrence and its restrictions, and substitutability and its restrictions.
(iii) 'Meaning' which falls within the range of linguistics will be at the level of *Form* and the interlevels of *Medium* and *Context*.

3.4.1 Hallidayan Functionalist Approach

Here we shall look mainly at the 'content'—both semantic and pragmatic. The Hallidayan functional view of language takes the semantic structure as the central point—not the formal structure consisting of certain abstract syntatic structures. A given utterance is viewed in terms of its 'meaning potential' and its lexicogrammatical actualization. The meaning (content) aspect is taken care of in terms of several functions and subfunctions. The following functions and sub-functions are postulated in Systemic Functional Grammar (See Halliday 1969, 1970 a: 324-7 and 1973; see also Chapter 24 in Halliday 2014; also Chapter 1 in Caffarel *et al.* 2004).

1. Ideational   (i)   Experiential
                      (ii) Logical
2. Interpersonal   (iii) Interactional (Rhetorical)
                      (iv) Attitudinal
3. Textual   (v)   Thematic
                      (vi) Informational

The concept of language function needs explication here. Halliday explains the multiple functions of language as follows: "A speech act involves selecting and putting into effect, simultaneously, a large number of multiple options from.... behavioural (but not 'behaviorist') stand point, whence language is seen as the potential and actual exploitation, at once creative and repetitive, of sets of socio-personal situations and settings, we may derive the notion of multiple function of language" (Halliday 1969).

Let's now explain these functions one by one. Here we have drawn heavily on several published and unpublished writings of Halliday.

The *Ideational* function of language combines two functions *experiential* and *logical*. Through the *experiential* sub-function the speaker is enabled to embody in language his experience of the real world, including the internal world of his own consciousness. The *logical* sub-function refers to the structuration of experience in terms of certain relations (e.g. sequentiality, consequentiality, hypotaxis, parataxis).

Interpersonal function is the function through which social groups are delimited, and the individual is identified and reinforced, in making interaction possible, language also serves in the expression and development of the personality. The *interactional* sub-function refers to the relationship between two interlocutors that is expressed in a speech act. On the other hand the attitudes of the speaker to the listener or the object of interlocution come under the ***attitudinal*** sub-function of language.

Textual function is the function whereby language serves to create texts. The ***thematic*** sub-function revolves round the concept of 'point of departure' for a given speech act. The ***informational*** sub-function revolves round the informational importance different blocks have in a given speech act.

The fact that language fulfills different functions is reflected in the organization of the grammar. Each function is expressed by one block of options. These blocks are called ***components of grammar***. The components of a grammar serve the functions of language and reflect the functions in the way they are organized. The components derive their names from the names of the functions they serve. The ideational component accounts for the expression of content, including, the persons, objects, abstractions, processes, qualities, states and relations that constitute the phenomena of experience (the experiential component) and, the abstract logical patterns related to experience though indirectly (the logical component).

The interpersonal component involves the hearer as an essential participant in the speech. The interactional sub-function gets reflected in this component of grammar in the form of mood, expressing sentence function in the sense of statement, question, command etc. The attitudinal sub-function gets reflected in different options—e.g. lexical items, intonation.

The textual component is concerned with the distribution of information in the clause, various forms of emphasis etc. This component is also relevant to the speaker-hearer relation, since it is his control over this part of the language system that enables the speaker to interact appropriately with his interlocutor, and to structurate what he is saying, through the various thematic and other options, in such a way as to construct dialogue.

Let's look at these functions from the viewpoint of what we have termed as 'semantic content' and 'pragmatic content'. Semantic content is expounded by the lexicogrammar and phonology of language. Pragmatic content on the other hand is derived on the basis of the background—sociocultural (wider situation) or (immediate) situational.

The experiential function of language with its participants, processes and circumstantials comes within the rubric of semantic content. The logical function also comes under semantic content as far as the directly expounded features are concerned. But once we take the help of our knowledge of the external world to talk of an implicit relation we are drawing on what we can call the 'pragmatic pool' (after 'presupposition pool' of Vennemann). Then that part of the content is pragmatic content. There are two interesting aspects to be discussed here. One, what is semantic in one context may be pragmatic in another context; and the other is that we can talk of the semantico-pragmatic threshold. (For a detailed discussion of Hallidayan approach on similar lines see Leech, 1983: 56-73.)

3.4.2 Sememes and Pragmemes

Let's talk of the semantic primes and pragmatic primes. The former are ***sememes*** and the latter are ***pragmemes*** (Prakasam 1986, 2004). *Whatever is 'denoted' by a lexical item directly will be a bundle of sememes and whatever is 'connoted'* *will be a cluster of pragmemes.* Here inferences and suggestions will be included. Let us take two pairs of lexical items:

**Master and *Slave*
Senior and *Junior.***

The lexeme 'slave' will have as one of its constituents the sememe [subservience]. On the other hand the lexeme 'junior' will not have it as its sememe. However, in certain contexts we might find a junior being expected to be subservient. In this case our information is from pragmeme [subservience]. In other words a given feature of content can be 'sememic' in one place and 'pragmemic' in another.

Let's look at the set of lexemes *Master, husband, father, friend* from the point of view of the feature [authority]. This feature will certainly be a sememe in the case of 'master' and a pragmeme in the case of 'friend'. Between these two clear points we have 'father' and 'husband' where [authority] seems to be the semantico-pragmatic threshold: it is partly sememic and partly pragmemic. Their sememic-pragmemic ratio may differ between the two words and across cultures. In some cultures [authority] might simply be a pragmeme in all the three words. One should of course keep in mind the problem of individual and societal variation regarding sememic and pragmemic values. It is very important to note that semantic change may consist mainly of interchange of sememes and pragmemes.

A pragmeme may operate at the rank of a lexeme or at the rank of a proposition. The study of pragmemes at the rank of lexeme may be considered lexical pragmatics and the study of pragmemes at the rank of proposition is propositional pragmatics. The pragmeme of [authority] has lexical origins.

On the other hand the feature [adult] is a propositional prag-meme used while comprehending the following sentence:

John voted for the liberals.

Let's now return to the functionalist viewpoint. The *interactional sub-function*, which takes care of 'mood' distinctions like interrogative and declarative, is semantic in nature because the relevant distinctions are 'worded' as it were—here 'wording' is used to include 'non-segmental phonologization' (prosodization) too. The attitudinal function which gets realized in the choice of lexical items and intonational features is also part of the semantic content. The textual function however seems to go in for both the 'pragmatic' and the 'semantic' rubrics. Wherever *extrasentential* or *extralinguistic* (phychological, cultural) reasons are to be brought in to explain certain choices we are within the pragmatic orchard. But on the other hand there are cases where certain lexicogrammatical and phonological features explain the thematic and informational choices—here we are within the semantic mansion. Here too one might be again on the threshold in certain cases. One thing is clear though. Some of the informational choices are overtly realized, but the triggering mechanism is not available in the immediate experience and is embedded in the sociocultural melieu. Here pragmatics certainly stakes its claim.

3.4.3 Presupposition, Entailment and Implication

We shall now try to look at three important concepts from the semantic and pragmatic grids:

Presupposition
Entailment
Implication

Let us examine the following sentence:
1. Mohan is a bachelor.
This sentence may be said to have the following meanings attendant on it:
(a) Mohan is of marriageable age.
(b) Mohan is an adult.
(c) Mohan is yet to get married.
(d) Mohan will get married.
(e) Mohan may get married.
(f) Mohan may be trying to get married.

(a) is a presupposition triggered by the lexicogrammatical structure of the sentence itself, because the word 'bachelor' refers to someone who is not married but could have been married. But the word does not tell us anything of the age at which someone in a given society gets married. That only an 'adult' gets married is part of sociocultural information. So (b) draws its information from the pragmatic pool: hence it is pragmatic presupposition; (c) more or less is like the 'assertion' part of the content. It is semantic entailment. The fact that he will get married (d) will be pragmatic entailment. That Mohan may get married is a legitimate aspect of futurology—hence it is semantic implication. The 'trying' part is not warranted by any part of the sentence; hence it is considered pragmatic implication. From (a) to (f) there seems to be a kind of sliding from the semantic pole to the pragmatic pole. The least semantic and the most pragmatic item is (f).

Bates rightly made the distinction between semantic and pragmatic presuppositions. There is a tendency among some to consider all presuppositions as pragmatic. What the code reflects is 'semantic' and what the encoder and decoder reflect is 'pragmatic'. This of course does not obliterate the threshold problem.

CHAPTER IV. Stylistics: Literary Semantics

4.1.0 Indian Poetics: An Overview

Here an attempt is being made to give a bird's eye view of (ancient) Indian Poetics to the extent it will be relevant to modern stylistics. Stylistics here is taken to refer to "the linguistic study of literature", keeping the aesthetic interpretation as the ultimate aim, which is also shared by different schools of literary criticism.

4.1.1 Bhāmaha

Bhamaha, a Sanskrit Literary theorist of the seventh century, defined poetry as follows:

śabdārthau sahitau kāvyam

That is, poetry is that in which "word and meaning coexist". In other words 'expression' and 'content' cohere in poetry—they are in unison here. This definition implies that a successful stylistic analysis of a poem will involve both expression and content. Such an approach constitutes an important aspect of literary criticism. On the other hand this implication of stylistics questions the value of bland statistical statements regarding the linguistic forms in a piece of literature. Some stylisticians have seriously objected to that kind of stylistics (O'Toole 1975: 176; 1976:1). Real stylistics, then, aims at literary appreciation through the text, the focus being on its linguistic aspects (cf Jakobson 1960) and Widdowson 1974: 116).

4.1.2 Rasa Theory

The different approaches to style briefly surveyed here are complementary and can be integrated into one comprehensive body of literary criticism. The theory of *Rasa* ('poetic emotion') mainly discusses the 'value' of poetry which gets actualized in the language of the poem(s). The value here is obviously aesthetic emotion. Being aesthetic, this becomes partly 'subjective' on the part of the reader. This is what Allan Tate says about poetry: "we read poetry as a special discipline, becoming scholarly about it or ecstatic about it according to our profession, temperament and mood" (1960:3). Oscar Wilde who treats a critic as an artist says: "the meaning of any beautiful created thing is at least as much in the soul of him who looks at it as it was in him who wrought it" (1921:144). *Rasa* however is not the figment of a reader's imagination, though his imagination and refinement are necessary to realize it. It incorporates also his instinctive reaction to certain objectively definable criteria that manifest or delineate or lead to the effect of *Rasa*. The disposition of a man is the outcome of the organization of varied instincts and emotions around one dominant instinct which in turn is developed round an object or idea. The different aspects of these poetic feelings and dispositions are no doubt to be found in the work itself, defined by the objects and situational contexts. This subjective-objective complex of *Rasa* is rightly considered the soul of poetry. This is embodied in or effected by several phenomena (see Chari 1976:287).

4.1.3 Dhvani Theory

"*Dhvani* is an exclusively poetic feature concerned with exploiting the beauty of every element in the medium of language....

to serve the ultimate artistic end of *rasa"* (Krishnamurti 1974:xxxi). This poetic feature consists in the suggestion of a sense beyond the literal or the metaphorical meanings of an expression. One may here be reminded of the "unheard melodies" being "sweeter", as Keats puts it. To deal with this aspect of meaning we have to extend our linguistic semantics. From this point of view we need to talk about at least the following types of meaning: denotation, extension, inference, connotation and suggestion. Suggestion has sometimes been considered the long range action of denotation. The other three may be considered as points between the two extreme points of denotation and suggestion. The poet's creative handling of words may be considered the main source of their suggestive power. This power may emanate from both the sense and the word itself. The latter with its phonological and formal properties functions as the source of suggestion. The suggestion may be code-based (semantic) or coder-based (pragmatic) or both. In other words it can be text-based or context-based or both. This suggestive power of language is part of what Jakobson terms the poetic function of language which is the dominant and determinant function of verbal arts (1960:356, cf Kuppuswami Sastri 1945:19). This indirectness or obliquity in literary semantics is reflected in E.M.W. Tillyard's comment: "all poetry is oblique: there is no direct poetry" (Krishnachaitanya 1965:119). Here by 'poetry' Tillyard obviously refers to 'good' poetry excluding mere verse or bad poetry.

4.1.4 Rīti

The School of *Riti* (style, manner, or mode) believes in the theory of a suitable arrangement of sound and sense for the purpose of producing poetic effect. The ancient Indian scholars speak of several styles which can be postulated on a cline between the two extremes – the limpid style and the ornate style. These styles are characterized by the way the web of words is spun to delineate emotions. Style is related to the temperament of the poet and the needs of the subject matter. It is here that the *Rasa* has its birth and the style reveals it to us. This aspect of literary criticism is discussed by Western critics under '(poetic) diction' (O'Toole 1974:2, Cf Korg 1959:32-44; also Wellek and Warren 1963: 179-80; see especially Longinus's *On the sublime).*

4.1.5 Auchitya

The essence of artistic expression is said to be *auchitya* (propriety) which is the proper placing of things semantic, syntactic, lexical and phonological in such a manner as to suit the desired poetic emotion or *effect (rasa)* and the avoiding of things not suitable. This propriety is harmony; it is proportion between the whole and the parts, between the chief and the subsidiary (Raghavan 1973: 217-8). This propriety also achieves 'unity' of a literary piece (see 4.2.5). This doctrine of fitness and literary propriety involving the need for sound and appropriate subject matter and the correct choice of diction and metre was discussed by Aristotle and especially by Horace. The latter expected every part and aspect of the literary work to be appropriate to the nature of work as a whole (Dorsch 1965:23). Longinus treats this propriety as one of the sources of sublimity in literature (ibid: 25). Lack of propriety (impropriety) is the real flaw in literature, Here impropriety is lack of integration of different elements. But the ancient Indian scholars also cautioned us against passing hasty judgments on the propriety of a literary work which has seemingly unintegrated or contradictory elements. The seeming contradiction or impropriety may after all be the actualization of what Brooks calls 'paradox'. He states that poets "work by contradiction and qualification" (1960:45). Propriety cannot therefore be decided upon absolutely. What determines the propriety of any literary category is the poetic context. Abhinavagupta, a Sanskrit scholar of the tenth century is categorical on this: "one cannot be indiscretely using the word propriety itself. Propriety is ununderstandable without something else to which things are appropriate. Propriety is a relation and that to which things are or should be in that relations must first be understood"— (Krishnachaitanya 1965:204).

4.1.6 Vakrokti

If *Rasa* is the ultimate of poetry, dhvani is the artistic process which 'evokes' it and 'aids' it; *Riti,* which can be taken to subsume *auchitya,* delineates it or 'expresses' it. It is here we can bring in an important theory of poetic expression. Modern linguists compare poetic expression with our day to day ('casual') speech and call the former 'deviant' from the latter. This 'deviance' concept has two implications: different from the 'favourite' (or 'normal') expression, or 'ungrammatical' and 'unacceptable' expression. We will establish in the course of our discussion that the first implication is the more positive and useful one than the latter. The second implication isn't really the common factor in poetic expression. Rabindranath Tagore refers to this phenomenon and makes a very interesting comment:

> When we come to literature we find that though it conforms to rules of grammar, it is yet a thing of joy, it is freedom itself. The beauty of a poem is bound by strict laws, yet is transcends them. The laws are its wings, they do not keep it weighed down; they carry it to freedom. Its form is in

law, but its spirit is in beauty. Law is a first step towards freedom and beauty is the complete liberation which stands and shines on the pedestal of law; (emphasis mine; Kuppuswami Sastri 1945:19).

When Bateson says (1971:59) that a poem provides him both a grammatical and a stylistic word order and that only the latter is the proper subject for literary comment, the stylistic word order has to be taken as grammatical but specially used in poetic expression. Once we free this 'deviance' concept from the implication of 'incorrectness', we are close to the concept of *vakrokti* ('peculiar' expression) used by Sanskrit therorists. Kuntaka, in the eleventh century, gave this concept primary importance and discussed all other concepts with reference to it. He explains this quality of poetic expression as the peculiar charm or strikingness which can be creatively donated to ordinary expression by the poet. This expression is also 'deviant', but it is so from the 'commonplace' expression, not from the 'grammatical norm'. The deviation is *vakrokti* only when it is effective in attaining strikingness. This speciality or 'peculiarity' of poetic expression may occur in the following cases (De 1961 xvxi-ii):

1. the arrangement of sounds (e.g. alliteration)
2. the choice of lexical categories
   (e.g. synonymy, descriptive adjective, compounds)
3. the choice of grammatical categories (e.g. voice, case, tense, number)
4. the organization of sentences (e.g. use of poetic figures)
5. the choice and development of a topic
6. the composition as a whole.

These six types of *vakratā* are incorporated in our discussion of different types of 'prominence' and 'coupling'.

As an instance of the peculiarity of the poetic expression, we can refer to the use in it of figures of speech. The figures used in poetry are usually classified as of two types: ideal figures (connected with idea) and verbal figures (connected with 'word'). Mammaṭa, a Sanskrit scholar of the eleventh century, suggests a test to distinguish these two types of figures: if the figure disappears with replacement of the word by its synonym, it is the verbal figure; if it doesn't it is the ideal figure (De 1960 vol. 2:72). In terms of current linguistic terminology, the ideal figures belong to the semantic stratum of language and verbal figures to the formal (phonological and morphological) stratum of language. Leech has made a distinction between phonological and formal figures : under the former he groups alliteration, rhyme, vowel harmony, assonance etc., and under the latter parallelism, anaphora, antistrophe, epanalepsis etc. (1955:147).

4.1.7 Svabhāvokti

An important concept that deserves mention in this context is *svabhāvokti.* the expression which is least deviant is called *svabhāva* (natural) *ukti* (expression) (Raghavan 1973:151-5). This naturalness is to be distinguished from the 'commonplace' expression. This concept was especially mentioned by Aristotle: "The greatest virtue of diction is to be clear without being commonplace" (Dorsch 1965:62). The charm or effectiveness of a thing as an object of a poet's description is achieved here without any embellishment. In other words it is an expression endowed with poetic power, without the ornament, This naturalness can also be taken to refer to the state where the *Proudhokti* (elevated expression) or *Vakrokti* does not sound artificial, involved or 'suffocated', This is what Longinus obviously meant when he said that a rhetorical figure would appear to be most effective when the fact that it is a figure is not apparent (Dorsch 1965:127). For him art is perfect when it looks like nature. This constraint is applicable to all aspects of expression including poetic figures.

4.1.8 Sahṛdaya

Let us conclude this brief survey, historical and comparative, with a note on 'critic'. In Sanskrit the critic is called *sahṛdaya* (someone with a sympathetic heart) or *rasika* (a person of 'taste'). The critic's experience is said to be a circuit starting with the poet and ending with himself since in his experience he indulges in aesthetic recreation (Raghavan 1973:138.335). Not every reader is a critic. He has got to 'mature' into one. The constant relishing of poetry refines the sensibility of the reader in such a way that cues can trigger the aesthetic experience. That is, he is not only expected to know the intricacies of theoretical requirements, but also to possess fine instincts of aesthetic enjoyment (De 1960 Vol.2: 43). Then the critic is primarily someone who has a sense of beauty. This idea can be seen well developed in several western theories too (See Kuppuswami Sastri 1945). A highly artistic attitude to critic is to be found in Oscar Wide (1921). His comments on the critic are very significant. He considers the distinction between creative faculty and critical faculty to be entirely arbitrary. He thinks that no creative act which involves the spirit of *choice* and subtle tact of *omission* can be possible without the creative faculty (121). He adds the there is no *art* where there is no style and no *style* where there is no *unity* (123; emphasis ours). For him criticism is really creative in the highest sense of the word. It is, in fact, both creative and independent (127). The highest criticism treats a work of art simply as a starting point for a new creation (143). He considers the 'beauty-sense' as the primary requisite for the critic, the temperament exquisitely susceptible to beauty, and to the various impressions that beauty can give us (194).

A real *sahṛdaya* with that beauty sense may not require any theory of stylistics to react the way he does to a literary piece. Stylistic categories he needs only when he wants to methodically explain his 'beautiful' reaction to others. The scholarly tools do add to and enrich our appreciation of a literary piece.

4.2.0 Functional Stylistics

Let's now work out a comprehensive model of 'stylistics' which builds in all the concepts relevant for appreciation of poetry. This is a literary stylistic model which "concentrates on the aesthetic purposes of every linguistic device, the way it serves a totality" (Wellek 1960:416).

"The hypotheses of criticism... are concerned with the shaping principles peculiar to poetic arts which account in any work for the power of its grammatical materials to move our opinions and feelings in such and such a way (Crane 1953: 169). The three most important principles we could consider the shaping principles of poetic arts are **prominence**, **unity** and **rhythm**. These three aspects belong to both content and the linguistic expression of a poem because they are in close contact and the former is 'implied' in the latter and is 'dependent' on it,

4.2.1 Prominence

Prominence as used here is an extended variety of 'foregrounding" of Mukarovsky (1970:43-7) and 'prominence' of Halliday. Halliday interprets foregrounding as 'motivated' prominence and prominence as "the phenomenon of linguistic highlighting, whereby some features of the languages of a text stand out in some way" (1973: 112-13). As we view poetry from Bhāmaha's point of view, quoted at the outset, we do take it for granted that prominence in poetry is 'motivated'. Before we explain our concept of prominence we have to make a distinction between two types of content: ***universe*** and ***thesis***. For example, the universe of Robert Herrick's To *Daffodils* and William Wordsworth's *The Daffodils* is the same. But these two poems differ as to their 'thesis', The thesis of a poem is its semantic interpretation (see Mukarovsky 1970, 48). Whenever we refer to the inseparability of content and expression we have thesis in view, not the universe. We cannot 'summarise' thesis – we can only 'interpret' it and 'appreciate' it. We cannot really appreciate universe — we can talk about it. Thesis is the secondary universe created by the poet whereas the primary universe is a 'given'. To summarise this difference:

Universe	**Thesis**
Given to the poet	created by the poet
Summarisable	non-summariable
....	object of interpretation
....	object of appreciation
Source material	finished product

The semantic interpretation of a poem obviously presupposes all the aspects of its expression too. The concept of prominence can be properly utilized only when we look at language from the functional point of view.

4.2.2 Markedness

To arrive at the complete thesis of a sentence, we have got to interpret it from all the angles. The concept of markedness is extremely significant here. An expression is marked for one or more phenomena—morphological, syntactic, lexical or semantic. An unmarked expression is used normally unless there is 'a good reason' not to do so (see Halliday 1970b: 159). The marked expression brings a particular feature or entity into prominence (see Verma 1976). This prominence is obviously semantic and structural. Consider the following:

1. Blondes he dates.
2. As regards blondes, he dates them.
3. He dates blondes.

Sentence (3) is (least marked or) unmarked because the usual word order (actually group sequence) is SVO in its neutral form. The unmarkedness of this simple sentence can be established on all the six axes mentioned above as (sub-) functions of language: (See 3:4:1).

1. S	V	O	
He/	dates	/ blondes	
Actor /	Process	/ Goal (?)	Experiential
theme	rheme		- thematic
Given	New		- informational
declarative pattern: statement			- interactional

This sentence is also 'unmarked' as regards logical and attitudinal axes, assuming that the speaker does not intend any extra meaning like irony, contrast etc., and that it does not imply any logical relation with any other text. On the other hand sentence (1) is 'thematically marked' since the theme of the declarative is not the subject:

O	S	V
1. Blondes	he	dates
theme	rheme	(thematically marked)

This thematic marking is neutralized when 'blondes' is made part of another clause (here minor) as in sentence:

2. As regards blondes,   he dates them.
   (minor) subordinate clause   main clause

A sentence is marked 'informationally' in English if the 'New' category (phonologically realized as tonic element) is occupying a position other than the last lexical position:

4. He dates **blondes**. (New : unmarked)
5. He **dates** blondes. (New : marked)

This can be 'demarked' by pronominalizing the last lexical item.

6. He **dates** them. (New : unmarked)

This phenomenon is self-evident. Pronominalization takes place when we know the referent which consequently does not expect or receive 'New' status. When both 'dating' and 'blondes' are 'given' they can be replaced by proforms or dropped.

7. Who dates blondes?
8. He does. (unmarked)

A sentence is marked as to its interactional function in cases like the following:

9. He dates blondes ? (+ Rise/Fall-rise tone) marked question

Sentence (9) has an 'affirmative' pattern (SVO, without any question word) used for a question. After all, this is an echo question meant to express one's doubt or surprise—not an information-seeking question like:

10. Does he date blondes? (unmarked question)

Consider the following:

11. Mohan went home and had a bath.
12. Mohan went home and then had a bath.

Sentence (12) is marked for 'sequentiality' where as (11) is not. This is logical markedness. Sentence (13) is marked for 'coordination':

13. Mohan and also Janardhan went home.

In English 'accompaniment' and 'instrumentality' are syncretised as in the following sentences:

14. She crossed the road with a stick. (instrument)
15. She crossed the road with her husband. (accompaniment)

These sentences are experientially unmarked.

The two semantic functions are made explicit in the following constructions:

16. She crossed the road using a stick.
17. She crossed the road along with her husband.

This distinction of 'markedness' is sufficient to establish that the linguistic markedness reflects semantic prominence. For an interesting discussion against 'markedness' see Haspelmath (2006).

4.2.3 Cohesion

Cohesion refers to relations of meaning that exist within a text (Halliday and Hasan 1976:4). It performs two functions: *marking prominence* and *forging unity*. When we refer to a particular semantic item by repeating a given word or by using pronouns or synonyms coreferential with it, we bring that semantic item into prominence. If we can, especially in a short poem isolate a particular semantic item (or 'sememe) by referring to the lexical items and other features, we get at the 'universe' of the poem. Hymes's 'summative' word and 'key' word are special cases of cohesion. He gives us three criteria in deciding the importance of words: (I) on the level of sound, containing sounds dominant in the poem and/or much higher in rank than usual; (2) on the level of meaning expressing the theme (universe) of the poems; (3) regarding position placed so as to have a culminating effect. He calls a word 'summative' when it meets all the three criteria and calls it a 'key' word if it meets only the first two criteria (Hymes 1960:118). It is important to remember that cohesion is achieved phonologically, lexically and syntactically *(cf.* Leech 1970:120-3).

4.2.4 Clustering, Collocation and Colligation

Prominence can also be achieved by handling the syntagmatic axis of language creatively. When two or more grammatical categories cooccur we say they *'colligate'*. When two or more lexical items cooccur we say they *'collocate'*. Similarly when two or more phonological items cooccur, they *'cluster.'* These three types of cooccurrence—***colligation, collocation and clustering***— can be categorized as to their expectancy as 'normal' and 'anormal' with several shades of normality in between. When the cooccurrence is on the side of 'anormal' we achieve prominence. Fudge has shown that 'anormal' cooccurrence of phonological features tend to increase the 'expressiveness' of the lexical items (1970:161). Let us consider the following examples:
  18. He walks (all alone) (on the beach).
  19. He walks the baby (every morning).
  20. He walks himself along the lonely path with great difficulty.
Sentence (20) is anormal because 'walk' does not take an object in general except when the object is an animal or a child or someone finding it difficult to walk. It never takes a reflexive object but in this sentence the use of 'himself' after walk has to be interpreted as we would interpret the role of 'baby' in sentence (19). The 'he' has to somehow 'pull

himself together' and 'push himself forward'. Here clearly the 'difficulty' is reinforced by using the reflexive object. The tension between the 'need' to walk and the 'inability' (mental and/or physical) to walk is reflected in the unusual colligation. Between the normal (18) (subject + verb intransitive) and the anormal (20) (subject + verb intransitive + object reflexive) stands (19) (subject + verb intransitive + object) where the intransitive verb has the marked function of 'causative'. The following are the instances of collocations and clusterings.

Collocations : sudden death (normal)
               delicious death (anormal)
Clusterings : *st*(op), *sq*(uash), *sn*(ail), *sl*(ide).

The effect brought about by clusterings can be considered as part of sound symbolism discussed by Hymes (1960:113).

We have already mentioned the use of *figures of speech* in literature. We cannot however ignore the fact that figures— both semantic and verbal— are used, nor infrequently, in common speech. The difference is only a matter of degree. Figures of speech help in achieving prominence. Phonological figures like rhyme and alliteration are also contributive to what Levin calls *memorabilty* (1962:58). Semantic figures including *ambiguity, indeterminacy, irony* and *pun* are contributive to the prominence of items within a poem. The figures especially mentioned above are exploited by poets to give more than one interpretation to their poems. This is part of their input. *Imagery,* which is the total effect we have of the figures, effects both prominence and unity.

4.2.5 Unity and Coupling

Levin rightly considers unity as one of the most significant aspects of poetry (1962:9). He postulates the concept of *coupling* as the key factor in achieving unity and memorabilty of a poem (p 33). For him coupling occurs when *'natural equivalence (phonic and/or semantic) converges with 'positional equivalence* (PP 29, 33, 39). Firth uses the term *parallelism* more or less in the sense of coupling (1951:196). We extend the principle to refer to the convergence of any two of the following equivalences:

(1) Lexical; (2) Semantic; (3) Syntactic; (4) Phonological (segmental); (5) Prosodic (non-segmental); (6) Figurative; (7) Metrical; (8) Positional

When more than two equivalences converge we have *reinforced coupling*. We shall call the single equivalence *semi-coupling*. These couplings effect the organization of a poem as a text (cf. Kelkar 1969:27-8). Cohesion by definition refers to the unity of the poem—semantic and formal. Coupling is an instance of cohesion. Though not with all the implications given here, coupling was considered one of the essential qualities of poetry by Sanskrit theoreticians. They called it *samatā* (parallelism or equivalence) and distinguished between *semantic samata* and *verbal samata*. This was discussed in detail by Vāmana in the eighth century (De 1960 Vol 2:94). Some critics considered the overdoing of samatā a defect (see also Levin 1962:48). These three types of coupling—coupling, semi-coupling and reinforced coupling—achieve prominence, unity and also rhythm. That's why Levin's emphasis on coupling is well placed though we can't agree with him when he says that coupling alone leads to memorabilty. Genuine memorabilty leading to contemplation is achieved by all the three shaping principles of poetry.

4.2.6 Rhythm

Rhythm adds to the unity of a poem and both unity and rhythm contribute to prominence which is the main tenet of our hypothesis of stylistics. Rhythm could be both external and internal—pertaining to expression and content respectively. Particular types of rhythm may be well suited to delineate the *rasa* (the poetic emotion) desired in the poem. This may also be part of sound symbolism. Semantic or ideational rhythm is chiefly achieved by the following:

(i) reinforcement of ideas
(ii) building up of an argument
(iii) imagery and figures of speech
(iv) coupling and cohesion.

Coupling is an important feature where quite often the semantic rhythm and phonic rhythm converge.

To sum up our hypothesis of stylistics we state that the three guiding principles of poetry are *prominence, unity* and *rhythm.* Though under rhythm we usually refer to metrical rhythm even the nonverse poetry rhythm will come under this. In this world border lines are never too clear. So the following cone may be postulated for different types of language from the literary point of view:

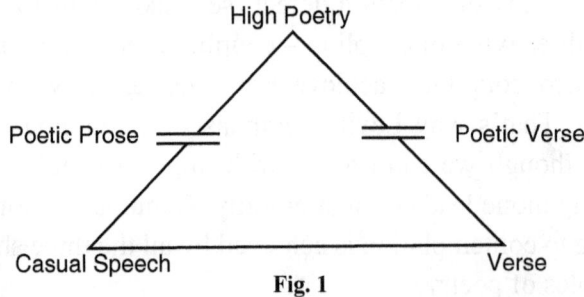

Fig. 1

As we move upwards, the three guiding principles acquire ascending importance. In high poetry we believe that all lead to 'prominence'. The primary axes along which we can discover these principles so as to account for the effect a poem has on us can be the following:

(i) functional prominence
(ii) cohesion, coupling, propriety
(iii) colligation, collocation and clustering
(iv) the thesis rhythm
(v) metrical pattern and its marked realization
    a) stress and its neutralization
    b) phonological figures
(vi) figures of speech — semantic and verbal

Rhythm is discussed in detail in the next section.

4.3.0 Metre and Rhythm

Rhythm adds to the unity of a poem and both together contribute to its prominence. Rhythm can be 'internal' (ideational or semantic) as well as 'external'. Here we restrict our attention to external rhythm. Metre and phonological figures are made use of to achieve the external rhythm of a literary piece. The external rhythm and melody concretise the prominent 'feeling' of a poem. Rhythm and melody are the products of thesis as well as metre. When thesis clashes with metre we get what is called *'counterpoint'* or *'tension'*. In this obviously the thesis has to win and consequently we get 'marked rhythm' which indicates for us semantic prominence. Sometimes the tension is between 'prose-rhythm' and 'thesis-rhythm' which accidentally may agree with metrical rhythm. We have then three types of rhythm:

1. Thesis rhythm
2. Metre rhythm
3. Prose rhythm

Thesis rhythm is marked rhythm and prose rhythm is its unmarked counterpart.

Coleridge mentions in his preface to ***Christabel*** that the poem runs on a new principle: in each line the accents will be only four though the syllables may vary from seven to twelve (Stauffer 1951:25). Abercrombie takes the seventy ninth line of the poem and tells us that there are only three accents on it:

My 'sire is of a 'noble 'line.

His analysis proposes a *silent ictus* to fill the gap (1964:10). But if we take the line in its context, we come up with an alternative interpretation. Christabel, a rich Baron's daughter, is frightened when she sees a 'richly clad' lady in the 'midnight wood'. She asks her who she is. Obviously the other lady observes the fright on Christabel's face. Sure she is that the lady questioning her is a rich lady. So she replies to Christabel reassuringly that she (too) is of a noble family. Here 'noble line' has to *be* considered 'given' (taken for granted) information in the context of the other lady being of 'noble line'. 'My sire' is 'theme' and does not qualify for being 'new' in this context. The reassurance comes from the fact that the strange lady's father also is a nobleman. So, for the purpose of emphasis *is* is the new element and bears the 'tonic' stress (sentence stress). This line constitutes a tone group with the tonic on 'is' which is marked 'new' information here. Thus the thesis rhythm wins over prose rhythm (which tells us that medial 'be' doesn't get stress) and agrees with metrical requirement:

My 'sire 'is of a 'noble 'line.

To restate our original standpoint, this is not a case of 'deviance', but only of marked stress, semantically motivated.

4.3.1 Metre Rhythm

The main ingredients of metre rhythm are stress, foot, line, stanza and phonological figures. A detailed discussion of phonological figures can be found in Chatman (1960: 152-3). We shall deal briefly with the other aspects. The phenomenon of 'stress' is here taken to mean the relative marked quality or quantity of a syllable—it can be a heavy syllable, an accented syllable or a long syllable (Lutz 1960:142). Metrical pattern spun around 'stress' has been defined from different angles. Thompson's stand that the metrical pattern imitates the structure of sound of the language is crucial for the existence of metre and the consequent rhythm (1970:337). Halle and Keyser postulate the concept of stress-maximum which they define as the linguistically determined stress (found in a syllable) that is greater than that of the two syllables adjacent to it in the same verse line (1970:381). This deals with the inherent word-stress as well as its environment. Taking into consideration their presentation of it and the later discussion of it by Beaver (1970) and Freeman (1970:427-91) we can consider the following as the important constituents of metre:

1. number of syllable positions in a line
2. density and distribution of stress maxima
3. neutralization of stress (when two stressed syllables occur in adjacent positions)
4. lexical stress neutralization
5. locus of stress neutralization
6. frequency of stress neutralization
7. character of the onset foot—weak, strong and reversed
8. diaresis, caesura, enjambment.

All these features depend to a large extent on the particular rhythm required and the consequent choice of metre. Any variation in the decided pattern may to a large extent be 'motivated'. Coleridge in the preface mentioned above says that the occasional variation in the number of syllables corresponds with 'some transition in the nature of the imagery or passion' (Stauffer 1951:25). All such variations are marked realizations of the metrical pattern of a poem.

4.3.2 Syllable and Foot

Syllable and its quantity are the primes of metre. The need for 'foot' in metre has often been questroned. Sometimes it has been given only heuristic value, not onotological status (Freeman 1970:335). We accept the position that foot is the unit of rhythm which repeats itself in the line. Besides its link with 'stress', foot has also a close relationship with the words used in the line. We can talk about diaresis where word boundary coincides with foot boundary. If we make a distinction between free word and bound word, the bound word will be part of the foot where the adjacent free word is the main element. Compounds operate as one foot whereas 'attributive + noun' phrases operate as two feet:

'blackbird *vs* 'black 'bird

The one important phonological aspect that hasn't been properly discussed in the theories of metre is the word boundary which is said to distinguish the following expressions:

night rate *vs* nitrate

If we can recognise foot-word parallelism (also syntactic phrase and phonological piece parallelism) with the help of certain phonetic features, we will be discovering an important aspect of rhythm. Chatman, in line with the skeptical tradition, says that foot boundary and word boundary may not coincide at all (1970:323). Such a situation might arise due to:

1. wrong scansion
2. bad verse (non-rhythmical) or
3. motivated variation

Sitapati argues with covincing evidence that even in a language like Telugu where 'stress' is not considered a very significant feature the diaeresis gives us better verse (1936).

4.3.3 Verse Line

The line is a well recognised unit of metre and to a large measure agrees with syntactic and semantic boundaries except when enjambment and caesura are in operation. Fowler describes the nature of a metrical line as follows: "The line is marked off, not only by the number of feet, stresses and syllables it contains, but by certain terminal bound features; perhaps by a pause, but more probably a prolongation of its last vowel and/or voiced consonant, often by a change in the pitch of the voice." He adds that the stanza (also a couplet) is identified by its rhyme scheme and often by a fall in the pitch of the voice at the end (1966:84). Here we have to bring in the concept of ***tone group*** (parallel to Trager and Smith's ***phonemic clause***). In an unmarked metrical line a tonegroup does not cover material from the next line. In other words the end of the line will coincide with the tonegroup boundary. When they don't coincide we have *enjambment.* if the tone-groups covering a line do not cohere together to constitute an utterance, we will have in the line more than one utterance (see for details Prakasam 1979). There we have *caesura.*

4.3.4 Synaloepha and Silent Ictus

Another important concept that needs explication here is *synaloepha*. Halle and Keyser state the circumstances for synaloepha as follows (1970:401): "Two vowels may constitute a single position provided that they adjoin, or are separated by a word boundary which may be followed by 'h'- and provided that atleast one of the vowels is a weakly stressed or unstressed vowel". Freeman has added /v/ and /d̪/ to this list (1970:453). Another concept which deserves to be brought in here is Abercrombie's *'silent ictus'* or *'silent stress'* which has an important role to play in explaining caesura or an occasional variation in a given metrical pattern (Abercrombie 1964). Most of the points discussed here will be illustrated in the next section.

4.4. Geralld Gould's 'Wander–Thirst'

We shall here examine a short poem by Gerald Gould within the frame work of the functional matrix worked out in the last two sections.

Wander-Thirst

Gerald Gould (1885-1936)

> I. Beyond the east the sunrise, beyond the west the sea,
> And east and west the wander-thirst that will not let me be;
> It works in me like madness, dear, to bid me say goodbye;
> For the seas call and the stars call, and oh! the call of the sky.
>
> II. I know not where the white road runs,
> nor what the blue hills are,
>
> But a man can have the sun for friend,
> and for his guide a star;

And there's no end of voyaging
when once the voice is heard,
For the river calls, and the road calls,
and oh! the call of a bird!
III. Yonder the long horizon lies, and there by night and day
The old ships draw to home again, the young ships sail away;
And come I may but go I must, and, if men ask you why,
You may put the blame on the stars and the sun and the white road and the sky.

4.5 Experiential Component

We shall look at the poem from the view point of functions of language. The experiential component identifies participants, circumstantials and processes. There are only two animate participants in the poem — the poet himself and a 'bird'. The third participant which could be interpreted as animate is the addressee — the 'dear' of the first stanza and the 'you' of the last stanza. The rest of the participants are inanimate. We can recognise the following *participant roles* and *circumstantials* for our analysis:

(i) causer/actor, affected (receiver/sufferer), goal (something or someone to be achieved/acted upon), object (a 'factual' phenomenon), attribute (qualifier) vocative (addressee) something uttered);
(ii) temporal, locative, manner;
(iii) processes are mainly of four types
State (x is in y); event (x fell into y);
action (z threw x into y); causation (z pushed x into y).

In the first stanza the following participant roles, circumstantials and processes are available:

Locative	:	beyond the east, beyond the west, east and west, in me.
Object	:	the sunrise, the sea, the wander-thirst that will not let me be, the call of the sky.
Object as actor	:	It, the seas, the stars
Vocative	:	goodbye, dear.
Affected	:	me (twice)
Manner	:	like madness
Causative process	:	to bid.... say, will not
Abstract action	:	works, call (twice), let

We can see that this stanza does not have single 'actor proper' role, nor 'action' proper. we have only abstract actions. The poet in all the three places mentioned is a 'me' either as a locative or as an affected. The causer/actor in all these instances is 'wander-thirst'. In the first case it does not 'allow' the poet to stay where he is. In the second case it is 'working' in him like madness. In the third case it is 'forcing' him to say goodbye.

'not let me be' ⇨ 'works in me' ⇨ 'bid me say goodbye'.

Though the third action is stated as the intention of 'wander-thirst' it is obvious it has succeeded in its aim. Now the poet is able to 'hear' the call of the seas, the call of the stars and the call of the sky. The wander-thirst has succeeded in making his 'latent' quest for the beyond' 'actual'. 'Logically' the last line of the stanza is the 'cause-specifer' for the poet's state of mind.

The last line of the stanza offers us an interesting case of marked colligation. The last clause—exclamatory and only of nominative material—is co-ordinated with two 'subject + verb' declarative clauses (see below). This syntactic markedness reflects the nature of the verb: 'call' is not so much of an action verb; it is more an 'object'. The S + V clauses from this angle be alternatively treated as noun phrases:

The/seas/call/(Determiner + Classifying noun + Head word)

This is not the syntactic structure available but the semantic structure emerging.

4.6 Interactional Component

Interactionally (in terms of speech functions like statement and question) all the clauses except two are declarative clauses making statements. One clause is a vocative: 'dear'. The other clause

'oh! call of the sky'

can be considered an interjection followed by an elliptical declarative clause. But its semantic prominence is better captured only if we consider it an 'exclamatory clause'. Attitudinally, the whole stanza expresses 'awe' and it is only proper that the last clause carries the burden of it. The choice of lexical items is also quite expressive. There are only five polysyllabic words in this stanza, the rest of them being monosyllabic words:

beyond, sunrise (compound), wander, madness, goodbye.

The polysyllabic words and quite a few monosyllabic words reflect the thesis effectively. The monosyllabic content words are:

east, west, sea(s), thirst, bid, call, stars, sky.

The other words are mainly (noncontent) structural words. The one monosyllabic word with only the nucleus vowel is 'oh' and it is expressive of the key semantic item 'awe'.

4.7 Summative Words

In this poem, we have to set up summative words for each stanza separately. In the first stanza the summative word is 'call'. We make this choice for several reasons;

   (i) It *sums up* the 'universe' of the stanza;
  (ii) It is placed in the last line and repeated three times;
 (iii) the two consonantal sounds 'k' and 'l' occur in the stanza each six times which is 'much higher in rank than usual,'

'Sky' and 'bid' can be treated the key words because 'sky' is the source of the 'call' and is as 'pervasive' as the wander-thirst itself and 'bid' reflects the forceful character of the call.

4.8 Textual Component

Textually the stanza offers us several instances of functional 'markedness'. The first three clauses are:

beyond the east (is) the sunrise

beyond the west (is) the sea

east and west (is) the wander-thirst

In these clauses the phrase sequence is:

locative phrase + object phrase

The usual phrase sequence in English will be just the reverse. This has two consequences: the locative phrases become the marked thematic elements and the objects get the new status. Locatives being the themes express the poet's state of mind;

he is talking not about objects but about the 'beyond' of his notional borders of perception (east and west). Once this is done, in the following lines the themes are the unmarked ones: it, seas, stars; 'to bid me' is a complex marked theme. Here the new elements are: 'like madness' 'say goodbye' call' and 'call'. The emphasis is obvious. The last clause in spite of being only mono-phrasal offers us the division:

theme: call; new: sky.

We shall realize in the next stanza that 'sky' is thematised though indirectly. This is part of the unity of the poem—the 'new' of the previous clause becoming the 'theme' of the following one.

The second stanza talks about the 'goalless' and 'endless' voyage the poet wants to undertake. The experiential roles found in this stanza are:

Affected	: I, a man (possessor)
Object	: white road, what, blue hills, the sun, a star, voyaging, the voice, the call of the bird.
Object as actor	: the river, the road
Goal	: for friends, for his guide
Qualifier	: no end
Locative	: where
Temporal	: when once the voice is heard
Processes	: stative: know, runs, are, can have, is heard; Abstract action: calls (twice)

As in the case of the first stanza we do not have a single actor-proper here. The one place where the poet is 'I', he is only the passive affected of the mental process 'know'. The 'white-road' must be the 'milky-way' which runs across the sky. It doesn't run in the active sense of the word. 'Blue hills' are the sky itself. Here he wants to say that he does not understand the nature and extent of the starry way. The verbs'–know, be, have, hear all are stative. The active verb 'call' is only that of an object and not of a real actor.

The last line offers us syntactic ambiguity:

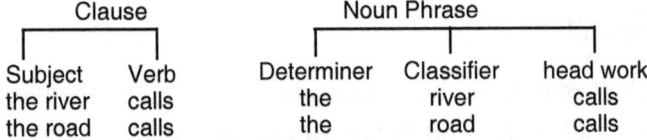

The second analysis yields us easier co-ordination with noun phrase: (oh) the call of a bird.

A comparison with the last line of the first stanza with its SV, SV pattern recommends an SV, SV analysis here too, An interesting number difference emerges between the two lines:

Line 4	Line 8
Seas (pl)	river (sg)
stars (pl)	road (sg)

The river and the road seem to be very close to the poet and are only means to reach the seas and observe the stars. His aim is not to travel on the roads nor row in the rivers. 'Road' may also be referring back to the 'white-road'. His goal is to go on an endless voyage on the (high) seas. For him the 'voice' is heard. Linies 5,6 and 7 give us a skyscape from where 'call' has come whereas line 8 tells us the immediate way he can choose—the roadway or the waterway. The 'bird' beckoning him to move out should be the 'bird of passage' flying the sky, covering thousands of miles and crossing several seas to migrate to a new home. This migratory bird may be posing a challenge to a man who is worried about his 'not knowing' nature well. The small bird may be helping him summon up his courage. The 'bird' is the only animate call-giver. it cannot be a particular bird the poet has in mind. It must be an object of nature being the exponent of the phenomenon of 'migration'; moreover it is 'a bird', not the bird'. The poet however is going to go out alone, but the sun is going to be his friend and a star his guide. 'But' is logically a co-ordinator, negating the implications of the previous clause(s). His ignorance about awe-inspiring objects of nature need not deter him from accepting the call to move out. The two polysyllabic words here are 'voyaging' and 'river' —one is the goal and the other is the means (see the section on metre). In this stanza once again 'call' is the summative word and the key words are 'voice' and 'bird'.

Textually the 'themes' and 'news' of this stanza are the following:

Themes: I, where, but a man, for his guide, there's no end, when once, the voice, the river, the road, the call.

News: know not, runs, are; the sun for friend, a star, of voyaging, (is) heard, calls (twice), of the bird.

We have already mentioned above that unity sometimes is achieved by transforming the preceding 'news' into the following 'themes'. 'Sky' was new in the last clause of the first stanza and is the theme of the third clause indirectly - 'blue hills': 'sky' is the source or location for most of the objects mentioned here. Its key position in the first stanza is thus further reinforced.

The third stanza refers to the inevitability of his moving out on a voyage. In the second stanza the emphasis was on skyscape and here it is on the seascape. Experientially we have the following categories:

Actor	:	I (twice), men, you
Affected	:	you
Object	:	the long horizon, the old ships (as actor), the young ships (as actors), the sun, the white road, the sky, (on) the stars (as locative)
Locative	:	yonder, there, to home, temporal: by night and day,
Manner	:	again (special use)
Process	:	draw (motion), sail away (motion) come (operating as object), go (operating as object), may put the blame (= may blame: abstract action); may (attitudinal functioning as mental process), must (attitudinal functioning as mental process).

In this stanza 'ships' are functioning as actors, later on to be compared with the poet himself. In two places 'I' (the poet/the wanderer) is the actor of attitude specifying verbal elements—'may' and 'must'. 'You' is the actor of the abstract action of blaming something or someone. Old ships draw to home 'again'. 'Again' reminds us of several things — they left the homes once, they may have come back once and gone again. By suggestion, even the old ones may leave again. The new ships are sailing away. The poet's going is a certainty (must) and his coming back is only a matter of probability (may). The objects of nature are to 'blame'. The long horizon lies within his sight (yonder) whereby he could observe the goings and comings of the ships. The certainty of his going may tell us that he is like the young ships. He is young and wander-thirsty. He is not just running away due to some conflict at home. He is being 'sailed' away by the objects of nature. The four polysyllabic words in this stanza are:

> yonder, horizon; again; away.

The first two tell us about the long horizon and the next two refer to going away again and again. After all, this is an endless voyage. From this point of view, 'again' is important logically. The other words logically important in this stanza are 'and' (line-initial of the third line) and 'but'. They are in equivalent place and contrasting with each other. 'Coming' is only a matter of 'sequence' and as a part of an ongoing activity—hence the sequential 'and'. On the other hand 'going' is most important for him and that has to be done now. This is the firm decision–hence the contrastive 'but'. There are only two occurrences of 'but' in this poem—in the second stanza and here. There it negates the implication of his 'ignorance' and here it expresses his decision to 'go' away. It looks as if we have progressed considerably from the first 'but' to the second one. The summative word in this stanza is 'blame' and the key words are 'must' and 'away'. The poet's being/going 'away' is a 'must' and he is not to 'blame' for this urge, but his youth (the passive receiver of the 'call' of the 'voice') and the great objects of nature (giving the call) are:

Textually, this stanza offers us significant instances of functional prominence. The 'themes' and 'news' are the following:

Themes: yonder (marked), by night and day (marked), the old ships, young ships, come (marked), go (marked), men, you.

News: horizon lies, again (marked), sail away, may (marked), must (marked), why, the stars, the sun, the white road, the sky.

In the poem the two instances of marked 'news' and marked 'themes' (all occurring in one line) which are of great importance for the thesis are:

come, go: marked themes

may, must: marked news

The poet is not talking about himself; he is just talking about two types of motion : coming and going. His announcement consists of the emphasis on the probability of his coming and certainty of his going. The two modal auxiliaries placed in the final position of the tonegroups (also clauses) for the reasons of thesis are given the tonic stress. In the reading of this stanza if we do not locate the tonic on 'may' and 'must' the stanza and thence the poem lose an important aspect of the thesis. Here the auxiliaries are functioning as full verbs of mental attitudes.

Before going on to the other aspects of the poem, we may say a few words about the 'dear' of the third line and the 'you' of the last line of the poem. It is possible the addressee is a woman. In the sixth line and the eleventh line there is the mention of 'man' and 'men' and both can be given the generic interpretation of 'human beings'. If viewed from this angle, after all, the addressee could be a pet or an object like the poet's house. This far we can go in stylistics. Beyond this we can go only if nontextual details are available and are taken into consideration.

4.9 Cohesion, Prominence and Unity

Let us now look at the poem from the point of view of cohesion and the consequent effect of prominence and unity. In this short poem there are in all 161 words. If we exclude the repeated occurrences of some of the items we have only 88 words used in this poem. Of these the grammatical items which enter into closed (finite) systems are 38. These items add to the thesis of the poem by modifying the meaning of the main lexical items or by stating their interrelationships. The repetition of 'the', 'and', 'but', 'for' and other items forge the unity of the poem. That's why they are called markers of cohesion. There are three classes of lexical (open) sets used in the poem; nouns, adjectives and verbs. The nouns are obviously those that refer to the objects of nature, and human institutions like 'friend' and 'guide' mostly relevant for travelling and 'voyaging'. The adjectives qualify the ships, the horizon and the objects of nature, and being only a few they do not give any 'descriptive' flavour to the poem. The three adjectives—old, young and long—are stative, not dynamic. Of the verbs many refer to 'states' or 'abstract actions'. The two motion verbs 'come' and 'go' function more like nouns. It is the verbal items of this type Halliday calls 'deverbalised' (1970c: 62). The preponderance of nominals and 'deverbalised' or nonaction verbals gives us the total effect of lack of action in this poem. This common semantic content of the words gives the poem its unity.

While talking about coupling we set up eight types of equivalences lexical, semantic, syntactic, phonological, figurative, metrical, prosodic and positional. There we mentioned three types of coupling: semi-coupling, coupling and reinforced coupling. Coupling, we have also said, is a type of cohesion. The very first line of the poem offers us a very good instance of reinforced coupling.

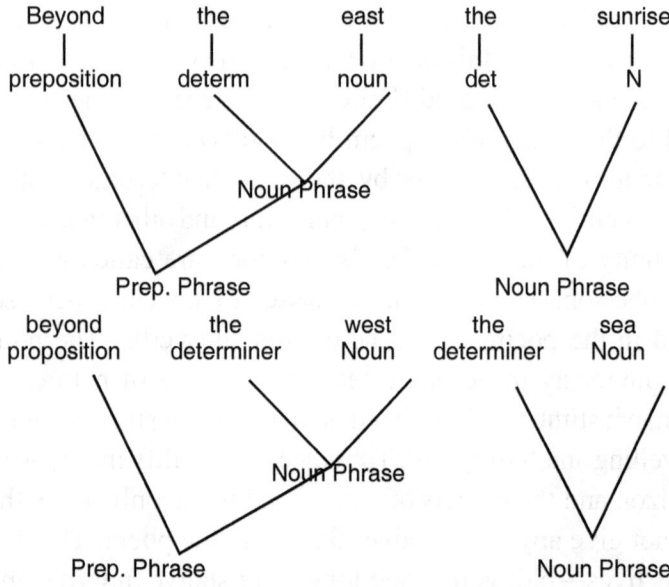

The two (i) initial positions are occupied by (ii) two prepositions which are actually (iii) two instances of the same word. When we come to 'east and 'west, (i) they are semantically of the same 'field'; (ii) they end with the same phonological cluster- 'st'. These two equivalences are reinforced by their positional equivalence. 'Sunrise' and 'sea' are (i) positionally equivalent, (ii) objects of the same 'semantic' field' of nature and (iii) have the same initial sound:'s'. *'Rhyme' by definition is coupling* because it has the *positional equivalence* converging with phonological equivalence :

'sea - be';   'bye - sky'   'are - star'
'heard - bird';   'day - away'   'why - sky'

Here this coupling is reinforced because of the semantic link the pairs have: 'sea' is one of the items disturbing his 'being' and 'sky' is one of the items bidding him say 'bye'. The call of the 'bird' is 'heard' and whether by night or 'day' the poet has to sail 'away'. 'Why' he wants to go away can be answered by only the 'sky' and its vast (sky) scape.

We shall take only one more important instance of reinforced coupling:

And	Come	I	may	but	go	I	must
conjunction	Main verb	pronoun as subject	auxiliary and marked new	same as 'and'	same as 'come'	same as previous 'I'	same as 'may'

Accidentally the initial consonants of 'come' and 'go' are the same except for 'voicing': they are dorso-velar stops, and 'may' and 'must' share the initial consonant (bilabial nasal). 'And' and 'but' are in a sense antonymous, 'come' and 'go' are antonymous motion verbs, and 'may' and 'must' are antonymous modals. This sentence can be set up as 'summative' sentence of the poem in terms of its thesis and coupling phenomena. This and other instances of coupling not only lend 'unity' of form to the poem but also unity of thesis.

The co-occurrence phenomena—colligation, collocation and clustering—add to the prominence of the poem, In the first line we have the structure of: Locative Prepositional Phrase + Subject Noun Phrase repeated twice without the stative 'be' between them. This is anormal colligation which may occur in poetry and also in response utterances. Similarly we have some anormal collocations like 'young ships'. Ships can be 'new' and animate beings can be 'young'. By using the anormal collocation the poet is suggesting the similarity between ships ad wanderers. The collocation 'white road' takes us off to the 'milky way'. Fudge says that the syllables in which the main initial and final consonants have the same place of articulation correlate highly with 'expressiveness'.

134 Semantics, Stylistics and Pedagogics

He also says that syllables beginning with a consonant cluster (especially when they also end in a cluster) are found in words which tend to be expressive like onomatopoeias, movement words, and prejoratives, jocular or intense connotations (1970: 161). We have a few words which come under this clustering:

star, sky, blue, friend, draw, blame

Thesis-wise, these words are 'expressive' in this poem.

4.10 Metrical Pattern of the Poem

Rhythm we have noted is mainly realized by the metrical pattern of a poem. To account for the metre of this poem which is iambic heptameter we can adopt Halle and Keyser' representation of the 'iambic pentameter' with a few modifications:

Principle 1. The imabic heptameter verse consists of fourteen positions to which may be appended one to four extra metrical positions.

Principle 2. A position is normally occupied by a single syllable but under certain conditions it may be occupied by more than one syllable or by none.

Principle 3. A stress maximum may only occupy even positions within a verse but not every position need be so occupied (see below).

The first line of the poem actualizes the metrical pattern in the following way:

Stress (5) Maxima		/ Beyond		/ the east		/ the sunrise		/ beyond		/ the west		the sea
Linguistic Stresses (6) Syllable positions (13)	1	/ 2	3	4	5	/ 6	7	8	/ 9	10	/ 11	12	/ 13

The important marked feature of this analysis is that the stress maxima are assigned to the ninth and eleventh positions which goes against principle 3. To fit the verse to this principle we can refer to 'synaloepha', (realization of one metrical position by two syllables) and say that the second occurrence of the 'beyond' should be taken to occupy only one metrical position (8). In this case we will have stress maximum only on position (10). We may suggest that 'beyond' undergoes the change because it is no longer important semantically. If we accept this position the metrical analysis of the line will be as follows:

/	/	/	⌢ /	/
Beyond	the east	the sunrise	beyond the west	the sea
1 2	3 4	5 6 7	8 9 10	11 12

This line gives us an anapaest (8,9,10) besides an amphibrach (5,6,7). Again to avoid this we can speak of synaloepha in the case of 'sunrise' and consider it as one metrical syllable (6). This would be stretching the concept too far. Another alternative is available if we accept Abercrombie's concept of *silent ictus* and place it after 'rise'. This gives us a very neat unmarked actualization of the metrical pattern:

/	/	/	/	/	/	/
Beyond	the east	the sun	rise ∧	beyond	the west	the sea
1 2	3 4	5 6	7 8	9 10	11 12	13 14

This Silent Ictus (∧) gives the line the required fourteen positions and the stress maxima are in the right (even) positions. The least satisfying alternative is the one which reduces 'sunrise' to one syllable position. The most satisfying solution will be the one with 'silent ictus' which occupies the eighth position in the line. This is also justified by the total pattern of the poem. Each line yields us two units: the first with 8 (or 9) positions (four feet) and the second with 6-10 syllables (3 or 4 feet). This is one of the two lines requiring silent ictus (see below). This is the only line which yields us two simple sentences, or two independent clauses brought together without any marker of coordination (see also line 10). Caesura is the most obvious and significant feature of this line. Finally we scan the line as follows:

(3 + 2)

/	/	/		/	/	
Beyond	the east	the sun	rise ∧ ‖	beyond	the west	the sea
/	/	/	/ ‖	/	/	/
1 2	3 4	5 6	7 8 ‖	9 10	11 12	13 14

Linguistic stresses: 4 + 3; Syllable positions: 8 + 6

The second line gives us a 'marked' realization.

(4 + 1)

/	/	/	/ ‖		/	
And east	and West	the wan	der thirst ‖	that will not	let me be

(4 + 3) /   /   /   /   /   /
(8 + 6) 1 2 | 3   4 | 5   6 | 7   8 ‖ 9   10   11 | 12   13   14

The dominant pattern of the poem is of fourteen syllables, six stresses and five stress maxima. The second line varies from it as regards the distribution of stress maxima and the nature of the last two feet (anapaests) and hence it is a 'marked' line. This is the line that gives us the title of the poem. So the markedness is justified by the thesis itself.

The third line has a marked 'foot'.

(3 + 2)

/		/		/ ‖ /		/	
it works	in me	like mad	ness dear	to bid	me say	good bye
(3 + 3)	/			/	/	/	/
(8 + 6) 1 2	3 4	5 6	7 8	9 10	11 12	13 14

The second foot here is not an iamb—it is pyrrhic. There is tension between the metrical pattern and actualization. The latter is dictated by the thesis rhythm; 'me' by its metrical position requires stress but semantically it is unimportant. This variation reflects the thesis—the poet as 'locus' for the workings of wander-thirst is deliberately played down. The alternative of taking 'me' as 'marked new' will not be unacceptable. The fourth line offers the phenomenon of stress neutralisaiton.

(0 + 2)

				‖ /	/	
For the	seas call	and the	stars call	and oh	the call	of the sky
(4 + 3)	/ /		/ /	/	/	/
(8 + 7) 1 2	3 4	5 6	7 8	9 10	11 12	13 14 15

In this line the second and fourth feet are spondaic and here the stress neutralization takes place from the stress maxima point of view. The first and the third feet are pyrrhic. The result is we have a weak onset. There are only two stress maxima—one on 'oh' and the other on 'call'. Both are significant words and so this marked stress maxima-actualization is thesis-wise justified. The last foot here is an anapaest.

The fifth line does not offer any marked features. The sixth line is marked.

138 Semantics, Stylistics and Pedagogics

(4 + 1)

/	/	/	/		/	
But a man	can have	the sun	for friend	and for	his guide	a star
/	/	/	/	/	/	/
1 2 3	4 5	6 7	8 9	10 11	12 13	14 15

Linguistic stresses: 4 + 2; **Syllable positions:** 9 + 6

Here the fifth foot is pyrrhic. The first foot is an anapaest and on account of this the stress maxima occupy positions 3,7,9 and 13-all odd positions. Rhythmically only the first foot is different. We should be *able* to reduce it to a two syllable foot to account for the unmarkedness of the rest of the line. Otherwise we have to revise the original principles regarding iambic heptameter saying that the stress maxima occupy only the last (*i.e*, the second) position in iambic feet. Then the position in the line becomes less important than the position in the foot. This further strengthens the general argument for foot—the unit which hypothesizes the recurring pattern of stressed and unstressed syllables that never exceed three in English (Beaver 1970: 437). If we reject the concept of foot we will not be able to account for our intuitive reaction to the unmarkedness of all the feet except the first in the line under discussion.

The seventh line is unmarked. The eighth line can be analysed in two different ways.

(2 + 2)

	/	/			/	/	
	For the river calls	and the	road calls	and oh	the call		of a bird
(4 + 3)	/	/	/	/	/	/	/
(8 + 7) 1 2	3 4	5 6	7 8	9 10	11	12	13 14 15

Linguistic stresses: 4 + 3; **Syllable positions:** 8 + 7

Excepting for the stress maxima and the feet constituency this line 'couples' fairly with the fourth line. The alternative analysis couple the two lines (4 and 8) completely:

```
(0 + 2)                                    /     /         /
        For the river calls and the road calls and oh  the call   of a bird
(4 + 3)          /     /   /   /   /   /          /      /           /
(8 + 7) 1  2     3     4   5   6   7   8      9  10  11  12     13  14  15
```

Linguistic stresses: 4 + 3; **Syllable positions:** 8 + 7

The stress neutralization phenomenon which operates in both the lines give them the slow effect which the thesis of the lines warrants (Freeman 1970: 463). In either analysis we have an instance or synaloepha.

Ninth line starts with a trochee and so here we have a reversed onset.

```
(3 + 2)
                /         /        /      /         /
        Yonder  the long  horizon  lies   and there  by night  and day
        /       /         /        /      /          /          /
        1  2    3   4     5  6  7  8      9   10     11  12    13  14
```

Linguistic stresses: 4 + 3; **Syllable positions:** 8 + 6

Besides this, there is an effect of sound symbolism in this line: all the linguistically stressed syllables have long vowels or diphthogs which give us the slow and 'dragging' effect which lines four and eight have due to stress neutralization. We can now take up the last line because the tenth and eleventh lines are 'unmarked' metrically. The last lines of the first and second stanzas (i.e lines four and eight) have fifteen syllables each – one more than the nonfinal lines. They have fewer stress maxima, due to stress neutralization. Here the last line has even more number of syllables.

(2 + 2)

		/		/
You may	put the	blame on	the stars

(2 + 3)
(8 + 10) 1 2 | 3 4 | 5 6 | 7 8 ‖

	/		/	
and the	sun	and the	white road	and the sky
	/		/	/
9 10	11	12 13	14 15	16 17 18

In this line only fourth foot is the regular iamb. The other feet offer us the other three types of feet we have had in the poem: pyrrhic, trochee, anapaest. This verse can be scanned in a different way:

(3 + 2)

/	/	/	/
You may	put the blame	on the stars ‖	and the sun
/	/	/	/
1 2	3 4 5	6 7 8	9 10 11

	/		
and the	white road	and the sky
	/	/
12 13	14 15	16 17 18

Linguistic stresses: 3 + 3, Syllable positions: 8 + 10

With its great variety of metrical actualization and the expressive word 'blame' and the complete skyscape recaptured, this line befits the role of being the last line of the poem. It is only here the poet speaks about wandering being a 'blameworthy' activity. Metrically and for giving us the list of 'culprits', this line is the most important one whereas the eleventh line is 'summative' of the poet's helplessness. With its variety of rhythm and a greater number of unstressed syllables the line moves even slower than the other two stanza-final lines. There are only six words in this poem which have initial consonant clusters:

> star, sky, blame, draw, blue, friend

Of the six words, the last line has three of them in it. Similarly all the dominant sounds and important words of the poem are found in this line.

4.11 Semantic Rhythm

We have said that semantic rhythm is achieved by reinforcement of ideas and building up of an argument besides cohesion and coupling. We have already noted while discussing the experiential function of the three stanzas of the poem that the thesis is well spun around the objects of nature, wander-thirst and the poet's helplessness. The thesis and variety of rhythm found in the other lines are reflected in the last line. This is what we meant when we said that rhythm adds to the unity and ultimately to the prominence of the poem. To sum up: the universe of the poem is one of 'quest for the beyond.' The poet has created his thesis in three stanzas. The first stanza of the poem states the problem the 'poet' is facing: he has got to say 'goodbye'. The second stanza expresses his 'ignorance' (I know not) about his goal. The third stanza tries to confirm and explain his urge to go away as a natural phenomenon attributable to the great objects of nature (and also perhaps to the exuberance of his youth).

CHAPTER V
Pedagogics: Meaning and the Language Teacher

5.1.0 Levels of Meaning

The third chapter gives us a fairly good picture of the levels of 'language analysis' where we have to discover meaning. To recapitulate it, we find meaning at the level of 'FORM' and the interlevels of 'MEDIUM' and 'CONTEXT'. So we have three types of meaning:

(i) Phonological or graphological meaning—significance
(ii) Formal meaning—value (lexical and grammatical)
(iii) Contextual meaning—content (semantic and pragmatic).

A good analysis of a piece of language will involve the discussion of these three modes of meaning. It has been the common practice of many linguists and teachers to deal with only the third type of meaning to the exclusion of the first two. The language teacher, especially when he is teaching a foreign language, will have to concern himself equally with all the modes of meaning. Otherwise his consideration of meaning will be a lopsided affair. As the Buddhist apoha theory suggests, a linguistic item has its significance by contrast and by exclusion of other related items. This phenomenon of contrast and non-self exclusion being common to all the levels of linguistic analysis, it is imperative for the language teacher to consider all facets of meaning.

5.1.1 Phonological Meaning

A consideration of phonological meaning at the outset will involve a clear understanding of the phonetic structure and

Chapter 5 ▪ Pedagogics: Meaning and the Language Teacher 143

phonological function of the phonematic units—their contrasts and distributions etc. Phonematic units are the phonological segments. We can also call them phonegments (Prakasam and Sodhi 1992). Next we will have to consider prosodic features which are 'supra' to phonematic units. In English 'word-stress' is a prosodic feature which plays a very important role in the intelligibility of one's speech. In Telugu 'y'—prosody before the syllable-initial front vowels, though not contrastive within the language, needs good consideration to help Telugu speakers avoid imposing it on English. For example, a Telugu student tends to pronounce 'ever' as */yevər/ and this should be rectified by contrasting L_1 with L_2. The units on the 'rank-scale' of phonological units are *phonegments (phonemic units) syllable, cluster, formative foot, tone-group* and *utterance* (see Prakasam, 1979, Prakasam and Sodhi 1992). **Phonegment is a phonological segment with its constituent features having static or dynamic values.** Formatives (clusters) are phonological counterparts of morphemes.

The 'supra' features of the tone-groups are covered by the term 'intonational' features which are spread over the 'utterance'. The supra features of 'syllable' and 'cluster' are covered by the 'prosodic' features. Sandhi features take care of phonological adjustments between clusters (formatives) when they are grouped into a foot. As a rule the phonematic unit doesn't have its supra features, unless as a part of the syllable in which case the feature will be ascribed to the syllable (see, however Prakasam, 1981). It will be difficult at present to come out with a clean picture of the units of graphology, but still we shall try to make out a few. We can deal with the graphational features /,/,/;/,/./,/?/ etc. quite easily. A careful study of these features will help the reader to a good extent to get at the intonational features. A teacher will have to decide the 'functions' or meanings of all the units and features discussed at the interlevel of medium. The units and features that are important for the consideration of meaning at the level of phonology can be presented in the form of a table as the following:

Table 1: The Phonological Hierarchy

Units	Features
Utterance } Tone group	Intonational
Foot	Sandhi
Cluster (formative) } Syllable	Prosodic
Phonegment	Static/dynamic

The units and features listed here for the alternate level of graphology are postulated keeping English in view. Other languages may demand different hierarchies.

Table 2: The Graphological hierarchy

Units	Features
Supersentence } Sentence } Clause	Graphational features
Group } Word	Grosodic features
Grapheme	Diacritics

Here, in the above Table 2, at least three terms need explicit interpretation. The Roman script as used for English does not employ necessary *grosodic* features corresponding to the prosodic ones. The IPA uses many such symbols and the Devanagari script uses several such marks for Sanskrit. By sentence is meant that utterance where the constituent clauses are closely knit and which is marked graphologically by marks such as /./,/;/,/:-/./ By supersentence is meant that unit of writing which is between two /. /s or between the blank space marking the beginning of a paragraph and the /./ at the end. This supersentence will be analysed at the phonological and grammatical levels through its constituents, i.e., the sentences (cf. Prakasam, 1985: 64).

5.1.2 Grammar and Lexis

At the two demi-levels of *grammar* and *lexis* (of the level of Form) the teacher will again come across different units at which he will have to consider meaning. The different *units* that are postulated for English at the level of grammar in the descending order of the rank-scale are *sentence, clause, group, word,* and *morpheme.* Each unit has its own structure and at each *element* of the *structure* of a given unit *operates* or functions a *class* of the unit next below. This relationship of an element of a structure and a class of unit is one of exponence or realization. A class is a grouping of items that function alike. A given class of items will yield further sub-classes when we make a move on the scale of delicacy, with a view to accounting for formal differences and the ensuing functional properties. The secondary classes obtained on the scale of delicacy make up *a system, which is a bundle of distinctive features—both formal and functional.* A discussion of the value of a grammatical unit involves a consideration of all these 'dimensions'. Here too we have to consider certain syntactic supra-features like 'word order'. Word order is of major importance for the study of the 'value' of English forms.

The lexical units we have tentatively postulated are *simple, compound* and *complex*. A statement of the meaning of a lexical item will involve a thorough consideration of the **nature** of the item, *its* **collocational span**, its **scatter**, and its membership in the **set**. As we have earlier noted, the full discussion of a formal item will mean its discussion at both the demi-levels of grammar and lexis from all the angles noted. For example the lexical item *'strong'* is a *simple node,* with the scatter *strong, strongly, strengthened,* etc., having on its span the collocates like *argue* and *tea* and entering into a set where other members will be 'power', 'force', and the like. Grammatically 'strong' is an adjective; it can function as a 'modifier' in a nominal group or a 'complement' in a clause.

5.1.3 Collocation and Colligation

A given piece of language will again have different effects depending on whether the collocations are *normal* or *anormal* or *casual,* whether the items which belong to the same set are often repeated or not and such criteria. For example the "Songs of Innocence" of Blake abound in items like 'golden', 'bright' and 'delightful' which can be assigned to the same *set.* Similarly a passage will have different effects depending on the choice of a particular grammatical item, its colligation, its repetition and the like. A story-teller achieves a positive effect, for example, by repeatedly using items from the system of 'cohesive' items like 'and', 'therefore', 'so' and 'but'. To sum up, it is obligatory on the part of the teacher to discuss the 'value'—both grammatical and lexical—of a piece of language he is set to teach.

It could then be fruitfully shown how in a passage the occurrences, co-occurrences and repetitions of items with certain value produce a specific effect. A good discussion of a literary piece will involve all such studies. A tabular representation of some of the categories of grammar and lexis for the discussion of meaning will look like the following:

Table 3

	Formal Level	
Demi-levels	Paradigmatic axix X	Syntagmatic axix Y
Grammar	System 1X	Colligation 1Y
Lexis	Set 2X	Collocation 2Y

At the grammatical level the meaning will have to be decided for the following units ranking on the hierarchical scale. These units are not universal' but 'descriptive' of English. Here they are given just as an illustration of what we mean by 'unit' and 'rank'. To put it in the form of a table:

Table 4: The Grammatical Hierarchy

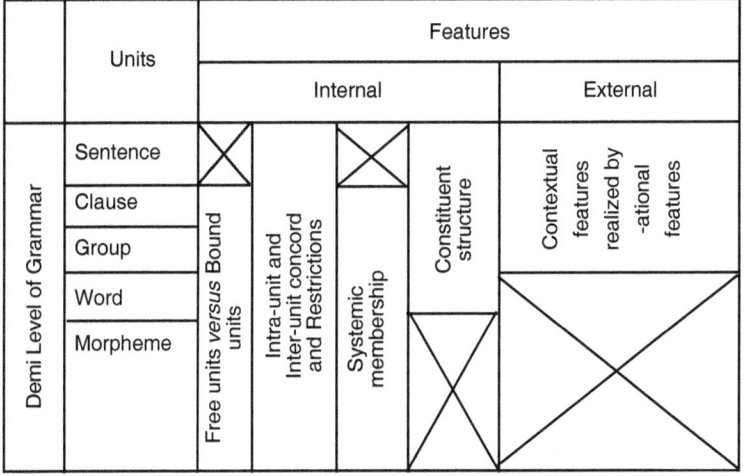

We can present lexical units and features in the following table:

Table 5

Units			Features	
Demi- level of lexis	Complex Compound Simple	Scatter	Set membership	Collocational span

5.1.4 Content

At the interlevel of context, as we have seen earlier, a specific type of 'meaning' will have to be discovered. This is the *contextual meaning* or *content*. 'Semantic content' is almost the same as 'meaning' in the common man's register and 'pragmatic content' is that part of 'message' which is not part of meaning. This content is the resultant of the interaction of 'formal' features and 'situational' features. In other words, a piece of language with certain (formal) values and (also phonological) significance will express certain content when placed in a particular situation. Here we wish to postulate a few tentative categories of content for pedagogic purposes. As noted above, content can be *potential* or *actual* (or instantial). The potential content of a language pattern is the sum total of the actual content of the occurrences of the same language pattern. In turn the actual content is an 'instance' of the potential content. On another dimension the 'content' of a language pattern is partly 'explicit' and partly 'implicit'. In other words part of the content is *denotative* and part of it is *connotative*. The connotative part differs from speaker to speaker and hearer to hearer. The 'implicit' part of the content accounts for figures of speech employed in speech.

On yet another dimension the content can be partly *rational* and partly *emotive*. The emotive part accounts for things like poetic emotion. On a different dimension we can say that the content is either *simple* or *complex*, the latter involving 'ambiguity' of one kind or the other and the former being unambiguous. From another angle the content can be *full*, that is, complete in itself, or *elliptical*, that is, demanding the content of language patterns not under direct consideration. Finally the content of an expression can either be *universal* or *particular* (the particular part of the content is that which is culturally determined).

A full picture of the content of a linguistic expression from all the angles noted above cannot be realized easily. But an attempt will have to be made in that direction. A lot of it could be achieved by treating the content from all the points of view of the features of situation. Something will still be unexplained due to certain subjective and inexplicable features, which we will have to leave off our picture. The category 'complex' is built in to note such features as well as those which make ambiguity appear unavoidable. A teacher will have to deal with all these factors and sort out the 'full' content with all sorts of help he can get from a given text, or cultural patterns of the people described in the text.

5.2.0 Conclusion for the Teacher

From the discussion we have had above, we will suggest that a language teacher should keep in mind the following conclusions:

1. 'Meaning' is of three types. A complete picture of the meaning of an utterance will involve the study of the three modes of meaning.

2. 'Phonological' and 'formal' meanings are particular to the language concerned.
3. The 'contextual' meaning is not that particular to the language community; it extends up to the social and cultural communities. Here again the 'content' of a statement might be 'universal' or `particular' to a religious or social or cultural community. For example, 'he ate his food' is a universal utterance whereas 'his engagement was announced' is particular to a cultural community.

Before a teacher takes upon himself the responsibility of explaining the 'meaning' of a given (linguistic) expression, he needs to remember quite a few facts about the language (See Nida, 1957). These facts have now reached the stage of over-quotation, but still they need mentioning:

1. All languages have the potentialities of describing and identifying all types of phenomena.
2. Different languages subdivide phenomena in quite different ways.
3. Forms reflect cultural differences.
4. Forms have areas of meaning.
5. There are no exact synonyms within a language.
6. There are no exact equivalents between languages.
7. When we *translate,* we translate an aspect of the area of content of a form of a language into another.
8. Ambiguities occur in all languages.
9. All languages exhibit changes in meanings of words.
10. To get a good and comprehensive picture of the meaning of an 'expression' in a language, we should not pose the question: "What does it mean?" but we should think in terms of: "How or when is this form used?"

Chapter 5 ▪ Pedagogics: Meaning and the Language Teacher

The world has different things for us to do and we have different ways of doing them. Each way is good for the purpose it is aimed to serve, of course if well handled. In the case of conveying meaning too—the phonological, the formal and the contextual—we have different ways of doing it. Generally whenever we think of meaning we have in view only the contextual one which in fact is preceded by the other two meanings. But it is also a fact that the first two meanings derive their existence from the distinctions made in the third one. The whole situation boils down to the fact that it is a constant process of mutual influencing. For a clear understanding of the phonological and the formal meanings of an item in a language, we have to consider the items operating in the network of phonological and formal relations of the language. This could be well handled by contrasting the network of the systems of the foreign language and the first language.

5.2.1 The Teaching of Meaning

The problem of conveying the contextual meaning is in fact a delicate and difficult problem. The meaning of even the so-called 'concrete nouns' and the words referring to tangible objects has to be conveyed very carefully and through different means. We also find that different means will have to be adopted at one and the same time to explain an expression. We can *semanticize* an expression, that is, give its situational meaning. We can *catenize,* that is, look at the patterns of the utterances, e.g. 'This is a book' and 'Is this a book?' Difference in meaning is conveyed here by (1) change in pattern, the words being the same, and (2) change in the intonation. We can also *contextualize* an expression verbally. These three approaches—semanticizing, catenizing and contextualizing—are from one angle. If we look at the problem from a different angle we may get at another set of methods of conveying the meaning of an expression. The three methods we shall discuss here are: (i) *translation* (interlingual), (ii) *interpretation* (intralingual), and (iii) *direct method.*

'Translation', as we have noted earlier, means to us recreation of the content of an expression of a language in terms of another language. For long, quite a few linguists and methodologists have raised their objections to using 'translation' as a technique of interpretation. But we can't justify any negative approach towards the very phenomenon. Proper handling of the technique might yield better results than its avoidance in the classroom. If one has to speak about the significance of /p/ in the phonology of English, he can nicely bring in the phonetically close sounds of the native language. If the native language is Telugu, the teacher can bring in the discussion of the two segments /p/ and /ph/ and contrast their significance in Telugu with that of /p/ in English, with its variants [p] and [ph]. This comparative presentation of facts can be done in the case of the formal meaning too.

If the teacher has to explain the value of a word, say, 'hand', he will introduce the Telugu word *ce:yi* and contrast their values. Here he will discuss the fact that *ce:yi* stands for both 'arm' and 'hand', and will further speak about the capacity of 'hand' to co-occur with 'in', 'over', etc. as in 'hand in' and 'hand over', and the absence of such colligational capacity in the case of *ce:yi*. This we can call *formal translation.* These two exercises of comparison are instances of (interlingual) translation. Next we come to *contextual translation.* This does not mean just giving a word-for-word equivalents as in some dictionaries. Here again a comparative presentation of the content of the words of the two languages is in question. If one could make the technique of translation quite rigorous and scientific it is a pious hope that the technique will do the maximum in a foreign language teaching situation. This technique has been used for long, sometimes misused and sometimes well-used. To sum up, what we mean by 'translation' is bilingual and comparative presentation of items. As a student comes with his native language, translation from L_1 to L_2 is more useful to pick up the new language.

'Interpretation' is intralingual whereas translation is interlingual. Some teachers choose interpretation of an utterance in simpler words but in the same language. This is more or less the same thing as Bloomfield's 'circumlocution' (1933: 140). If the given utterance cannot be understood by the reader because it is outside his experience span, the simpler interpretation should be within his experience and should fit the context. This seems to be a good and useful method, where translation is not necessary and where we don't waste time in intralingual interpretation. This method is pretty difficult till the intermediate stage of language learning and pretty easy and good for advanced learners. It has been found from experience that trying to explain grammatical categories intralingually up to the intermediate stage of language learning is less profitable than the method of *comparative presentation.* This comparative method gives us what we can call 'Translation Grammar Method' which is of great use at all levels (Prakasam 2010, Shiny 2016: 36-37). However, for the intermediate learners to a certain extent and for the advanced learners to a good extent, the intralingual interpretation helps the students feel well exposed to the active use of the foreign language. This makes them internalize the language and *think* in the language. This kind of intralingual interpretation holds good to the meaning at all the three levels.

Direct method by definition excludes the use of the mother tongue in a foreign language teaching situation. In this method, the teacher tries to establish correlatives between the physical world and the linguistic world in a *direct* manner. This too implies intralingual interpretation and seeks to *create coordinate bilinguals* (see glossary). The direct method has been quite popular for a few decades. It is now that the educationists are realizing that a strict adherence to the direct method, with the exclusion of the native tongue in the classroom, is not fruitful and so some judicious use of the native tongue is recommended. Many modifications of this sort have been introduced into the direct method at different periods. It is important to note, however, that no simple method or approach can exclusively be adhered to; we have to choose a method so as to suit the situation and the need.

5.2.2 Problems of Meaning

A teacher should be acquainted with all the noted techniques to teach a foreign language effectively. He will find quite a few problems which deserve his special attention. Some of the problems he would face are these: *ambiguities, abstractions, figures of speech, cultural restrictions, connotations.* These problems demand a discussion here.

By *ambiguity* we mean the phenomenon where we can observe any *verbal nuance*, however slight, which gives room for *alternative reactions to the same piece of language.* Here we refer to Empson's treatise on ambiguity (1953). *The first* type of ambiguity that Empson notes is one concerned with literature. A poet means more to us by an expression than an ordinary speaker with the same expression. When a poet uses similes or metaphors, we cannot say which side of similarity between two items is specially stressed by him and so there is an ambiguity in that. "Clearly this is involved in all such richness and heightening of effect, and the mechanizations of ambiguity are among the very roots of poetry" (ibid., p. 3). Here we have to note that we cannot perceive any *formal ambiguity* but only *content ambiguity*. A teacher then will have to disambiguate the expression with the help of the full knowledge of the literary piece, the literary writer, the atmosphere in which the writer was born and grew up and the like. This type of ambiguity includes a great many literary devices.

The *second* type of ambiguity Empson notes is one that occurs when *two or more meanings are resolved into one expression* (ibid., p. 48). Such ambiguity is the resultant of formal ambiguity, lexical and/or grammatical. This kind of ambiguity has to be solved formally first. Even if the lexical item is capable of more than one meaning in isolation, it will certainly yield a definite meaning if the verbal and non-verbal environment is fully considered. In speech the ambiguity in content is very many times solved by taking recourse to phonological patterns. In the written form we have to depend on graphological patterns. But we will now and then come across the instances where no such help will be available. Then we will have to account for the ambiguity by giving the utterance two types of Indian grammatical analysis. For example, the oft-quoted expression can be analysed as follows:

Flying planes can be dangerous.

1.	Subject (Demoted clause)	Predicator	Complement
Flying	planes	can be	dangerous
Predicator	Complement		

2.	Subject	Predicator	Complement
Flying	planes	can be	dangerous
Modifier	head word		

Figure 1

The *third* type of ambiguity occurs when two ideas, which are connected only by being both relevant in the context, can be given in one word simultaneously (ibid., 102). This in fact is the *intended ambiguity,* and so no more ambiguous, when the different meanings are intended to be read into an expression.

An ambiguity of the *fourth* type occurs when two or more meanings of a statement do not agree among themselves, but combine to make clear a more *complicated state of mind in the author* (ibid., 133). In this type of ambiguity the distinction will be more subtle, the pun more vivid, the mixture of modes more puzzling than in the third type. This ambiguity seems to be inevitable.

The *fifth* type of ambiguity again is one that is not grammatically or lexically engendered (ibid., 155). It occurs when the author is *discovering his idea in the act of writing,* or not holding it all in his mind at once, so that, for instance, there is simile which applies to nothing exactly, but lies half-way between two things when the author is moving from one to the other. Here the ambiguity is one that is puzzling and difficult to understand.

The *sixth* type of ambiguity occurs when a statement says nothing, by tautology, by contradiction, or by irrelevant statements, so that the reader is forced to invent statements of his own and they are liable to contradict one another (ibid., 176).

The *seventh* type of ambiguity Empson notes is similar to the fourth one. This occurs when the two meanings of an expression, the two values of the ambiguity, are the two opposite meanings defined by the context, so that the total effect is to show a *fundamental division in the writer's mind* (ibid., 192).

5.3.1 Abstraction, Figures of Speech and Cultural Milieu

Abstractions are an important part of thinking since they are a means of revealing relations imperceptible to the senses. A few basic concepts about abstractions are worth mentioning here:

(1) Students must be made aware that they abstract and classify, thus emphasizing similarities and obscuring differences.
(2) Students should learn to distinguish report from inference.
(3) They should learn to recognize that definitions are nearly always partial and tentative.
(4) Students should learn to think in terms of multiple values rather than only two.

Then the teacher will have to keep all these points in view when he handles abstractions, classifications, definitions, etc.

Different *figures of speech* are found employed in all types of written and spoken material. It is quite natural for human speech to be indirect in what is needed to be said. A teacher will have to handle these figures intelligently; otherwise he would make the students feel that 'figures' are unnecessary ornaments. As an exemplification of our statement we shall discuss *metaphor*. When a teacher wants to handle a metaphor in an interesting manner he can keep these ideas in mind:

(1) Metaphor is made up of the *vehicle,* which is the subject or action that carries the meaning of the metaphor and the *tenor* which is the meaning of metaphor.
(2) The purpose of using a metaphor may be to express likeness or unlikeness, or to point out characteristics of the object talked about, or to startle or shock by the juxtaposition of violently different items.
(3) Metaphor is an integral aspect of language, a chief means by which words are given new meanings.

If metaphor is handled in this way, it not only teaches the youngsters something about language but also aids in a successful approach to poetry. This type of systematic approach to any other 'figure' is an essential technique to teach a language effectively. Figures like dramatic irony, hyperbole, and simile demand a careful and fascinating treatment on similar lines.

In spite of all the commonness in the life of different nations and races, plenty of differences can be observed in their cultures. Language, being an expression of culture, gets in some areas highly particularized in the content. For example many idioms and phrases reflect quite closely the *cultural patterns.* In other words, the full realization of a linguistic expression demands the understanding of the cultural implication the expression has for the native speakers. So Wilga Rivers makes the following assumption: "The meanings which the words of a language have for the native speaker can be learned only in a matrix of allusions to the culture of people who speak that language" (1965). A corollary to this assumption is: "In order to use a foreign language effectively the student must learn to use categories in the same way as the native speaker if he is to avoid false impressions and frequent misunderstandings." This aspect is dealt with in detail by Robert Lado in his *Linguistics Across Cultures*. Lado – but here it is worth noting that a matrix of allusion to another culture cannot help the student to comprehend the content of language unless their selection and presentation are most carefully analysed in the light of 'meanings' which will be imposed by the culture of the learners. To gain growing comprehension and a deepening apprehension of cultural meanings one has to undertake wide reading where words are met in the variety of contexts. This 'wide reading' is imperative for the teachers of foreign languages.

A good knowledge of the culture of the native speakers help the teacher and the learner to distinguish the *connotation* of an expression from its *denotation*. Connotation contains a large element of emotion, e.g. anxiety, whereas denotation refers particularly to visual and factual effects. Denotation amounts to the 'rational' content and connotation to the 'emotive' content. The 'emotive' content is more in literacy pieces than in non-literary pieces. A teacher will have to take all these points into consideration to do full justice to the explanation of an expression.

5.3.2 Summary

The following is a summing up of the main points raised and discussed in this chapter:

(1) Meaning has to be described and analysed at the level of 'Form' and the interlevels of 'Medium' and 'Context'. It

is a product of a network of complex functions performed by different units and features of the given level or interlevel.

(2) Meaning can be conveyed in different ways, depending on the *stage of learning,* the *purpose of learning* and other such criteria.

(3) No single method of conveying meaning will be successful in all the teaching situations. Different methods like translation, interpretation and direct method, and semanticization, catenization and contextualization should be made use of as the need arises.

(4) A teacher will face different problems which he will have to handle very carefully by adopting different standards and methods of teaching.

Glossary

Abhihitānvaya vāda: The theory which propounds that words convey only the individual word-meanings and that their mutual relation is conveyed by the word-meanings, not by the words themselves.

Abstractions: Abstractions are part of our cognitive process and they reveal relationships imperceptible to the senses.

Accent: The emphasis with which a given syllable is spoken relative to the adjacent syllables; also called stress. Rhythm is the result of accentual patterns of a given utterance. In this book we have spoken of three types of rhythm. **Prose rhythm** is effected by what are called 'lexical' accents which are inherent. **Thesis rhythm** is effected by what are called 'rhetorical' accents triggered by the need of a context. **Metrical rhythm** is effected by metrical accents, required by the rules of the verse pattern chosen.

Action: One of the process types, the others being **state**, **event**, **causation**. Halliday postulates three main process types for modern English: Action, Mental Process, and Relation. According to Chafe an action verb expresses an activity, something which someone does. It is accompanied by an agent noun.

Actor: The participant who performs an 'action', *e.g.* I ran away.

Adhyāhāra: The elliptical sentence where the syntactic expectancy is not fully satisfied; on the other hand, vākyaśeṣa refers to the incompleteness of a syntactically complete sentence.

Agent: Instigator of the action and typically animate identified by the verb, *e.g.*, I ran the machine.

Ākāṅkṣā: The desire or requirement of an individual word or words in the sentence for others to complete the meaning. This factor distinguishes a sentence from a string of words (cf. valence).

Akhaṇḍapakṣā: The synthetic method; the theory according to which the fundamental linguistic fact is the sentence. Bhartṛhari considered sentence as "a single integral symbol".

Ākṛti: The generic shape.

Alliteration: The repetition of sounds or syllables in two or more words of a verse line or of a cluster of verse lines.

Ambiguity: The phenomenon of double or multiple signification. Ambiguity could be lexical or grammatical, e.g.:
Bank (river bank, money bank—lexical);
Visiting professors can be expensive (syntactic):
(a) Professors visiting us can be expensive.
(b) Visiting professors can be expensive for us.
Ambiguity could be *pragmatic, e.g.,* Six wives of Henry VIII.
To someone from a society where polygamy is allowed, it could mean he had all the six wives at the same time; to an Englishman, he married six women, each time after divorcing the previous wife.

Amphibrach: A foot consisting of a long syllable placed between two short syllables.

Analogists: Those Greek thinkers who believed that there was a logical relationship between meaning and the words of their language.

Analyticity: The phenomenon of the predicate expressing one of the properties of the subject, *e.g.,* Wives are women.
Such expressions are also invariably true. They are therefore called tautologies (cf. syntheticity).

Anapaest: A foot of 2 short syllables followed by 1 long one.

Anaphora: The repetition of the same word or words at the beginning of several utterances.

Anekaśabda Darśana: The theory that explains polysemy as a phenomenon of "many words with the same sound pattern" (homonymy).

Anomalists: Those Greek thinkers who believed that the relationship between words and their meanings was irregular and arbitrary.

Anomaly: Contrary to an acceptable pattern; can be broadened to mean 'deviance', 'incorrectness' and 'unacceptability'.
Phonological anomaly:
'Beged' for 'begd'.
Graphological anomaly:
'Storys' for 'stories'.
Morphological anomaly:
'Unregular' for 'irregular'.
Syntactic anomaly:

*This my request.
*They is coming home.
Lexical anomaly:
'Light coffee' for 'weak coffee'.
Semantic anomaly:
She is John's *father.*
Pragmatic anomaly:
He got into the empty gin bottle.

Apparent anomalies may get deanomalized in specialized contexts.

Antistrophe: The repetition of the word or phrase at the end of several utterances.

Antonymy: The phenomenon of semantic opposition; incompatibility of meanings; the opposition could be on different dimensions:
Sex: Cow × bull; boy × girl; actor × actress.
Age: Man × boy; woman × girl.
Proximity: Here × there; now × then.
(See Contraries, Converses, Contraditories.)

Anumāna: Inference.

Anvitābhidānavāda: The theory which propounds that both individual word-meanings and their mutual relation are conveyed by the words themselves.

Apoha: The Buddhist theory of meaning according to which the essence of meaning is negative in character. The meaning of a word is a conceptual image whose essence is positive qualified by the negation of all its counter-correlates.

Āptavākya: The direct statement of a trustworthy authority.

Apūrvata: The novelty of the subject matter; this is one of the indicators which help us obtain tātparya' (purpose of a passage).

Argument: Argument is one of the two constituent elements of a proposition, the other being 'predicate'. Arguments are entities which are related to one another by predicates.

Arthapatti: Postulation

Assertion: This term is sometimes used as a synonym of 'proposition'. It is also used to refer to the main aspect of the meaning of a word. For example the sememe 'unmarried' is considered the 'assertion' in the word 'bachelor' and 'male' and 'adult' as part of its presupposition; a positive statement *vis-a-vis* negation (*e.g.* He is a teacher *vs* He is not a teacher).

Assonance: The vowel identity, especially in the stressed syllables and also in the succeeding unstressed syllables in a verse line or in a cluster of verse lines.

Assumption: The act of assuming something to be true.

Asyndeton: The omission of conjunctions, articles and pronouns to achieve effects of economy and speed.

Attitudinal: Concerning the attitudes of the speaker to the listener or the topic of discourse.

Auchiti: Propriety or congruity (will help us choose the right meaning).

Auchitya: Propriety; the proper placing of poetic material so as to produce the desired effect.

Autonomous Syntax: Also known as 'Interpretive Semantics', or the 'Standard Theory of Generative Grammar'. It is propounded that the syntactic component of the grammar is independent, *i.e.* autonomous of semantics. In other words, the factors which determine the grammaticality of a sentence operate without reference to those which determine the meaning of the sentence.

Background Entailment: The entailment which gives us the new element. For example, *John painted something* is the background entailment of *John painted a car*.

Back Reference: Reference to an item already mentioned by using the same item again or by using a synonym, a definite article, or a pronoun, or elliptically, referring to the context.

Beneficiary/Benefactive: The semantic role of one that is 'benefited' in a technical sense, *e.g.*,
    Anu made him *a cup* of coffee.
This is different from *dative, e.g.*,
    Anu gave him a cup of coffee.
Sometimes 'beneficiary' is referred to as 'ethical dative'. Chafe uses the term beneficiary to cases as following:
    Sam has a car.
    Anu bought *Sam* a car.

He uses the term 'benefactive' for verbs of 'have' and 'buy' type.

Caesura: A pause or break within a verse line.

Case Grammar: The linguistic theory which proposes to treat semantic roles like agent and dative as the primitives of the deep syntactico-semantic structure. Fillmore's model recognizes deep cases (K) and surface cases. For each verb a case frame is proposed to tell us how many and what type of nominals it goes with. This is like one-argument or two-argument predicate. Anderson's case grammar (1971) has *localist* orientation. Pāṇṇini's *Kāraka theory* anticipates the modern models. Hornby's and Palmer's (H.E. Palmer) models of verb patterns anticipate the case frame concept.

Catenize: Study an expression in terms of patterns in which it occurs.

Causative: A verb is called a causative verb when it causes to bring about a new state, causes an event, or causes an action. An 'event' verb itself will be causing a change of state. An 'action' verb might cause a change of 'state' or cause an 'event'. Causation might be fused with another non-causal element or it might assume a discrete position. This variation might also show difference in meaning:

> Mary *is* in the kitchen (state).
> I *left* her in the kitchen (causation of a state).
> Mary *went* into the kitchen (action).
> I *sent* her into the kitchen (causation of an action).
> I *made* her *go* into the kitchen (discrete causation).

Many linguists derive transitive verbs from intransitives & by causative process. For example, in English, 'die' and 'kill' are related to each other by causal relationship though they are not morphologically related as in Hindi *mər* (to die) and *mār* (to kill).

Circumstantials: The items expressing the concepts of time, space and manner.

Cluster and Configuration: Weinreich uses the term 'cluster' to refer to a grouping of features which can be taken in any order. For example, the features 'female' and 'offspring' given for 'daughter' can be taken in any order. On the other hand in the case of a 'configuration', the features are to be taken in a set order. For example, the features 'furniture' and 'sitting' are to be taken in that order for the word 'chair'. Leech proposes the term 'cluster' for a unit to be placed between 'feature' and 'predication'. The cluster is a unit which consists of features and which enter into relations of hyponymy and incompatibility; the cluster is the unit of language which has the property of referring: the relation between a cluster and reality is 'denotation' or 'reference' (Leech, 1974; 128).

Clustering: Cooccurrence of sounds.

Code: A system of signals used for communication (includes linguistic signals).

Cognitions and Concepts: Cognitions are phenomena like images, mental ideas and particular thoughts which form part of the conscious experience of an individual. They are individuated in part by the individual. Cognitions are datable. Concepts are abstract entities. They do not belong to the conscious experience of the individual. They are the objective content of thought process, which is the common property of several thinkers. Concepts are not datable (Katz: 1966).

Cohesion and Coherence: Cohersion is the phenomenon of linkage across phrases, clauses, sentences and paragraphs. Coherence is semantic linkage.

Colligation: Co-occurrence of grammatical categories; colligation can be 'normal' or 'anormal'. For example, an 'intransitive action verb' does not colligate with an 'extensive complement (object)'. When it does, the verb has causative value. When it occurs with a reflexive complement it is more unusual and has literary value, e.g.,
   He walked all the way.
   He walked his horse.
   He walked himself along the lonely path.

Collocation: Co-occurrence of lexical items. Collocation could be 'normal' or 'anormal', e.g.,
   Sudden death (normal).
   Delicious death (anormal).

Comitative: The case role signifying accompaniment, e.g.,
   She crossed the road *with* her husband.

Comment: The part of a clause which talks about the 'topic'.

Communicative: Lyons says that a signal is communicative if it is intended by the sender to make the receiver aware of something of which he was not previously aware.

Competence: The knowledge a speaker has about his language. Communicative competence includes (linguistic) competence and also knowledge about the (appropriate) use of language. In a wider sense it refers to the system of rules that a native speaker has mastered so that he is able to recognize grammatical mistakes and ambiguities. It is an idealized conception of language, which is seen in opposition to the notion of *Performance,* the specific utterances of speech.

Complement: A major constituent of sentence or clause structure which is traditionally associated with 'completing' the action specified by *the verb.* In a broader sense, the term covers all obligatory features of the *predicate* other than the verb.

Componential Analysis: Decomposing a lexical item in terms of basic semantic components.

Connotation: The part of the message an expression conveys besides its denotative meaning.

Connotative Predicates: Predicates like 'even', 'still', 'only', 'also', 'already', etc., which besides transmitting the basic information content of the utterance also explicate the connotative meaning.

Consonance: The repetition of consonants in syllables and words in a verse line or in a cluster of verse lines.

Constative: Constative utterance is the expression Austin uses for declarative utterance (statement).

Construct Grammar: The grammar which is a cybernetic model and which represents a hypothesis about the structure of 'objective grammar' (Shaumyan 1977).

Content: The meaning of language at the level of context. The level that links lexicogrammar and situation.

Context: The interlevel between Form and Situation. In general use it is used to refer to specific parts of an utterance (or text) near or adjacent to a unit which is the focus of attention.

Contradiction/Contradictoriness: 'My *sister* has *no siblings*' is considered a contradiction because 'my sister' posits a sibling relationship between 'I' and 'sister' and this is contradicted by the predication 'has *no* siblings'. Such sentences are taken by Katz to illustrate contradictory sentence. On the other hand, contradiction is said to be reflected in inconsistent predication, *e.g.*,
   She *whispered loudly*.
   Here 'whisper' and 'loudly' contradict each other.

Contradictories/Contraries/Converses: These are instances of antonyms.
   Contradictories admit a range which stretches between two polar qualities, e.g. mortal/ immortal; regular/irregular.
   Contraries admit of possibilities between them and beyond them, *e.g.*, rich/poor; warm/cool.
   Converses: husband/wife; buy/sell.
   Sentences of the following type are conversely related:
   x gave y to z.
   z received y from x.

Conversational Implicature: An implication that can be derived from a sentence indirectly, in a given context, *e.g.*,
   Q. Will he help you in this regard?
   A. He is a snob.

The answer implies that *he* will not help because he is a snob. In other words a conversational implicature is an assumption made over and above the meaning of a sentence.

Cooperative Principle: This is Grice's hypothesis which subsumes a number of maxims specifying the conventions normally obeyed by participants in a given speech situation. These maxims concern quantity, quality, relation and manner in which speech event takes place. If a given speaker flouts a maxim, he is conveying some extra information which is called an 'implicature'.

Coordinate Bilinguals: Those who attribute partly or wholly different meanings to corresponding lexical units in the two languages—a distinction is being made with *compound bilingualism,* where the meanings are seen as identical.

Coreference: Reference by two or more items to the same object, person, etc., is coreference. For example, in the sentence *John* lost *his* way, 'he' in 'his' and 'John' are coreferential.

Context: Verbal context; in 'back and forth' – 'and forth' is the context of 'back' (of vākyaśeṣa).

Counterpoint: The deviation from the chosen metrical pattern.

Coupling: Convergene of equivalences: phonological, prosodic, lexical, morphological, syntactic, lexical, figurative, metrical.

Dactyl: A foot consisting of a long syllable followed by two short ones.

Dative: The semantic case identified by Fillmore as the case of animate being affected by the state or action identified by the verb.

Deep Structure: The syntactic/semantic/syntactico-semantic structure which is an abstract representation of relations and functions. Different grammarians use this term to suit different structural configurations.

Deep Word-Form: The word-forms that have a global representation, with no indication of the division into morphemes. Attached to each deep word-form is an index formed from the symbols denoting the syntactically determined morphological characteristics of that deep word-form.

Deixis: The system of reference to participants and circumstantials, *e.g., the* book
my pen
this teacher.

Denotation: The literal referential meaning of an expression.

Dhvani: Suggestion; suggested meaning leading to aesthetic relish.

Dialect (Geolect): The language variety decided mainly on the basis of the regional affiliation of the speaker.

Diaeresis: The coincidence of a word boundary with the foot boundary (especially with reference to their endings).

Discourse: A continuous stretch of language which can be represented on the semantic level as a single unit of a close-knit constituent.

Some linguists use 'text' for this concept and use 'discourse' for a given stretch of language.

Effability: Katz says this principle was first suggested by Frege. He explains the principle as follows: "anything which is thinkable is communicable through some sentence of a natural language (because the structure of sentences mirrors the structure of thoughts)". Searle's 'expressibility' and Tarski's 'universality' are comparable concepts.

Ekaśabda Darśana: The theory that "explains polysemy as a phenomenon of one word with different meanings".

Elision: The omission or blurring of a final vowel.

Ellipsis: Omission of a recoverable expression. The omission might be of a word, a phrase or a clause.
1. The omission could be due to its recoverability from the context. For *e.g.*,
   A. Are you going tomorrow?
   B. Yes, 1 am.
2. Sometimes the recoverability is from the immediate physical context. For *e.g.*, (to the milkman)
   "Two litres, please."
3. It could also be from the experiential background of the speech community, *e.g.*,
   (a) snake! (kill it!)
   (b) coffee! (bring it!).
   'a'—snake is to be feared/killed etc.; 'b'—coffee to be offered.

Emotive Meaning: That part of meaning which expresses one's emotions, attitudes.

Entailment: The relationship between two sentences under which S_2 follows necessarily from S_i because of a specific semantic relation:
   'He is an idiot' (entails).
   'He is not intelligent'.
   'Caesar died' (entails).
   'Someone died'.
   'She snubbed him for being insolent' (entails).
   'She believed/assumed that he was insolent'.
   'She left the place on Monday' (entails).
   'She was in that place before Monday'.

Two sentences are said to be in 'entailment' relation under the following circumstances:

S_1 S_2
True   True
False   True or False
Then S_1 entails S_2.

Enjambment: The carrying over of a grammatical unit from one line to the next.

Environmental: The socio-cultural aspect of the situation which provides the 'pragmatic pool'.

Epanalepsis: The repetition of a word or words after an intervening word or words.

Episememe: Constructional meaning whose effect is to make the meaning of a syntactic construction more than the sum of the meanings of its constituents alone.

Equivalence: See paralliesism

Ergative (ergativity): A term used in the grammatical description of some languages, such as Eskimo, Basque and Hindi, where a term is needed to handle constructions where there is a formal parallel between the object of a transitive verb and the subject of an intransitive one. For *e.g.*, He opened the door; the door opened.

In English, verbs which can be used transitively and intransitively are called ergativerbs.

Euphony: The quality of having smooth-flowing sounds which also sound pleasant.

Experiencer: The semantic role of a participant that accompanies an experiential verb, the one who undergoes an experience.

She likes grey-haired men.

Here 'she' is experiencer. Experiential verbs are *see, hear, feel, learn, remember, want, know, like,* etc.

Experiential: The function whereby language serves to express our experience of the phenomena of the 'real world', including the inner world of our own consciousness.

Exponence: The relationship of realization between an element of a structure and a term in a system, between a type and a token, between a category and an instance.

Extension: The extended use of a word for other than its strict referent; a certain sememe is isolated and the word is used for a referent possessing that quality, e.g., He is a fish (He drinks like a fish). This is primary extension. The secondary extension is from the use of the word for a wider reference area, e.g. In one sense whale is a fish.

Felicity Conditions: The conditions that 'felicitate a speech act'. For example, to request Y to do something (Z),
(i) X must want Y to do Z and must assume things about Y which will felicitate his utterance;
(ii) Y is able to do Z;
(iii) Y is not unwilling to do Z, if asked;
(iv) Y will not do Z, unless asked.
These conditions are also called 'happiness conditions' or 'preparatory conditions'.

Field Semantics: The superordinate area where many subordinate features could be subsumed.

Focus: The importance a word gets in a sentence in terms of its informational value. When a word gets the focus it is semantically the 'new' information and phonologically it receives the 'tonic' stress.

Focus of Contrast: The item selected by the speaker from a limited set of possible candidates as the correct choice for the focus.

Foot: A measurable unit of rhythm.

Foregrounding: Motivated prominence.

Form: The level of language which comprises the two demi-levels of lexis and grammar. This term is used by Hjelmslev, to refer to the pattern imposed by a language on content substance or expression substance (Hjelmslev 1953).

Fulfilling Condition: The condition of *covetive* type of proposition. A covetive type of proposition expresses a wish.

Functions of Language: The functions a language is called upon to perform. Different linguists identify them in different ways, Leech talks of five functions of language:
Function   *(Orientation)*
Informational (subject-matter)

Expressive	(speaker/writer)
Directive	(listener/reader)
Phatic	(channel of communication)
Aesthetic	(message).

Buhler postulates three functions:

Conative	(social control)
Expressive	(emotive)
Representational	(situational reality)

Halliday talks of three functions:

Ideational	(situational reality)
Interpersonal	(social /communicative reality)
Textual	(verbal organisation)

Halliday's contribution in this regard has been to establish the need of the multi-functional view of language, *i.e.*, a speech act contains some element of each of the three functions.

Generative Semantics: The linguistic theory which propounds the view that the semantic representation of a sentence constitutes its deep structure. It propagates that the syntactic structure should emanate from the semantic structure without the mediation of the syntactic deep structure. In other words it does away with one 'Interpretive Semantic' component. In this approach the semantic structure is given as a set of structures with semantic features as the constituents.

Fillmore's case grammar envisages a semantic deep structure as order-free representation and specified as to deep casal categorial relations between verb and nouns.

Chafe proposes a semantic structure as an assemblage of meaning configurations where relations matter, not sequentiality.

Genotype Language: The genotype language is a hypothesis about the general semiotic basis of natural language; it is a system of universal linguistic categories (Shaumyan).

Global Rule: A derivational constraint which relates non-consecutive stages of a derivation.

Goal: The end point of the movement of an object in the case of movement verbs. It identifies the final stage into which an object develops into in the case of 'state of change' verbs.

Grammatical Categories: Items belonging to closed classes of items, words or features, *e.g.* prepositions, pronouns, tense features.

Graphational Features: The graphological marks reflecting the semantic values of phrase-markers (parallel to intonational features).

Grosodic Features: The graphological marks reflecting prosodic features.

Hedgeword: A word used to avoid making a statement which can be considered incorrect or inappropriate, *e.g.*, technically, strictly, loosely speaking, sort of, kind of, regular, and real.

Heptameter: A line of seven feet.

Homography/Homonymy/Homophony: Homonymy is the phenomenon of two or more words having the same pronunciation and/or spelling, *e.g.*, bank (river); bank (money). Sameness of only pronunciation is also called 'homophony'; 'homography' refers to sameness of spelling. For example; 'see' and 'sea' (homophony); 'lead' (V) and 'lead' (N) (homography).

Hyperbole: A figure of speech consisting of exaggeration.

Hyponymy: Meaning inclusion; if one meaning configuration contains all the features present in another meaning configuration the relationship of hyponymy exists. 'Man' is hyponymous to 'grown up', 'male'. 'Subordinate' is used as a synonym of 'hyponym' to refer to the specific term and the more general term is called 'superordinate'.

Hypotaxis: Hypotactic relation refers to a relation of dependence. A hypotactic structure is a chain of dependences. The relation among different elements of a hypotactic structure is 'non-transitive' 1-2, 2-3, but not 1-3 or 1 (2 (3).

For example,
(1) I'd have given it
(2) if you'd asked for it
(3) before 1 sold it.

(3) is subordinate to (2) and together they are subordinated to (1) (cf. parataxis).

Iamb: A foot of a short (unaccented) syllable followed by a long (accented) one.

Ictus: Beat; the stressed syllable position.

Ideal: Concerning idea (meaning).

Ideational: The aspect of language or grammar which combines the experiential and logical aspects.

Idiom: A mutually sense-selecting construction, where each member has a sense that is possible only in construction with another item (Weinreich); an expression which has a meaning different from the meanings of its constituents; semantically *an* idiom behaves like one lexical item but grammatically the constituents behave like common words. For example,
    Kick the bucket (die).
    Kicked *the* bucket.
    *Kick the bucketed.

Illocution: The intention specifying force or *act;* an *illocution* is the conventional social act or ordering, advising, urging, etc.; it requires the intentional social act of ordering, advising, urging, etc.; *it* requires the intentional use of a conventional signal to carry out some socially recognized function. An illocutionary act is signalled by intonation, the mood of the verb, the presence of an explicit performative verb, etc.

Implication: This concept is being given rather a new value here. Presupposition has a 'pre'-value and *entailment* has a 'post-value when compared to a given *assertion.* Implication is that part of meaning which coexists with assertion, but not the assertion itself. For example, the sentence
Mohan is *a bright student.*
presupposes that (i) Mohan is student, and entails,
(ii) Mohan's brightness as a student is recognized by the speaker, and implies that
(iii) Mohan is *not weak* as a student.

Implicature: The extra information which one has to work out from sentences which somehow violate the Cooperative Principle, It looks as though 'Implicature' is a product of 'opacity' or 'rnetaphoricity' (cf. implication).
Conventional implicatures are those which are not truth-conditional, but which are not contradictable.
General conversational implicatures are common accompaniments to the meaning of a sentence but they can be contradicted.

Inchoative: Chafe uses this term for a semantic unit which converts a lexical unit of one type into a lexical unit of another type, e.g., widen = wide + *en*

The term is also used in the grammatical analysis of verbs, to refer to a type of aspectual relationship in which the beginning of an action is specified.

Inclusion: A superordinate feature like 'flower' is included in the subordinate item 'rose'. In another sense the specific 'rose' is included in the generic 'flower'. (cf. hyponymy).

Inconsistency: Contradictoriness across different propositions. For example,
(a) He *has come* here.
(b) He *went back*.
If (b) is true (a) is false; (c) will be true:
(c) He came here.

Indeterminacy: Vagueness of reference or categorization.

Inference: The part of (extended) meaning arrived at by reasoning and deduction.

Informational: Concerning the importance of different message blocks.

Informative: Lyons says that a signal is informative if it makes the receiver of the signal aware of something he was not previously aware (cf. communicative).

Initial Phrase-Marker: Chomsky (1975) prefers to use the expression 'initial phrase-marker' (instead of 'deep structure') for the structure generated by the base component of the syntax.

Interpretive Semantics: See Autonomous syntax.

Instrument(al): *inanimate* object or force causally involved in the action or state identified by the verb, as well as the stimulus or immediate physical cause of an event. For example,
He chopped the onions with a sharp *knife*.

Institutional Demi-level: The demi-level of situation which provides the background for the discussion of language variation.
    Jāti: The universal (type).

Interactional: Concerning the speaker-hearer relationship encompassing interactional and attitudinal.

Khaṇḍapakṣha: The analytical method according to which a word is an autonomous unit of thought and sense, and language studies are made on the basis of words, and the sentence is taken as the concatenation of words.

Lakṣaṇā: The indirect relation between the word and the meaning which is based on the similarity or contiguity of the actual intended sense with the original, primary sense.

Lexeme: The unit of semantic hierarchy which can be decomposed into sememes. Lexemes occur in the structures of arguments and predicates which occur in the structure of a proposition.

Lexical Items: Items belonging to open classes of words, *e.g.* Noun, Verb.

Linga: 'Indication'; gender; conventional meaning of a word.

Linking Coordination: Weinreich uses the term to refer to a construction which is composed of those semantic features which form a cluster.

Locative: The semantic case which identifies the location or spatial orientation of the state or action identified by the verb.

Locutionary: Concerning the referential or cognitive meaning.

Logical Function: Concerning abstract (logical) relations among different units of experience; *e.g.*, hypotaxis, parataxis, sequentiality, consequentiality. This is a subfunction of ideational function.

Madhyama: One of the three stages in the manifestation of the speech principle—the utterance in its phonological structure, the sound pattern of the form. It is psychological in its nature and can be comprehended by the intellect. All the elements linguistically relevant to the sentence are present in a latent form at this stage. This corresponds to Prākṛtadhvani.

Markedness: The phenomenon of being explicitly marked for a category or process; The phenomenon of marking something as 'plus feature' as opposed to its absence ('minus' feature). It can also be anormality *vis-a-vis* normality.

Medium: The interlevel between substance and form (Abercrombie).

Metaphor: Metaphor is an instance of semantic transfer; its non-literal signification arises out of the fact that a metaphor involves a violation of selectional restriction. For example,
They *killed* the *proposal.*
Here 'kill' is metaphorical; the sentence is non metaphorical only when its object is [+ANIMATE].
The figurative use of a word or expression to some other word to which it does not normally apply. No specific term of similarity (like) is used and a total identity between two unrelated items espoused.

Metre: The measurable rhymical patterns manifested in verse.

Metonymy: The use of the name of one thing in place of something that it symbolizes, *e.g.*, 'crown' for 'king'.

Metonymy: Substitution of one word for another; especially using abstract terms to express concrete concepts;

Modality: The sentential constituent (cf. Fillmore's Case Grammar) which includes such modalities on the sentence as a whole as negation, tense, mood, and aspect.

Myth: A body of symbols used to reflect certain opaque aspects of human or superhuman existence. Men need a 'myth' to unify their experience and writers use a myth to present their assessment of facts in an imaginative way.

Nānārtha Śabda: Polysemous word.

Narrative Poem: A poem which narrates a story (*e.g.*, epic, ballad).

Negation: Making a negative of a positive element of structure; the scope of negation is an important factor in the structuration of one's choice. For example,
(a) All went home
  can have two negatives depending on the scope of negative.
(b) *All* did *not* go home (some did).
(c) *None* went home.
Givón makes the following points about negatives:
(1) Negatives are used to correct misguided belief on the assumption of the hearer's error.
(2) Negatives presuppose the knowledge of the corresponding affirmatives.

It is important to note that we cannot start a discourse negating a word of 'negative' quality. For example,
*"Solomon was not a bad king."
"Solomon was not a good king."

New: This concept is similar to the Indian concept of 'vidheya'. Halliday introduced this concept into modern linguistics in 1957 but developed it well in 1967-68. This refers to the important aspect of the information structure, phonologically expounded as tonic stress. Chafe 1970 defines it as "what the speaker assumes he is introducing with the addressee's consciousness by what he says."

Nucleus: The main element of a structure.

Objective Grammar: The logical mechanism stored in the speaker's brain; it exists only in human consciousness, but is treated as an object independent of man.

Octameter: A line of 8 feet.

Octave: A cluster of 8 lines. The first eight lines of a sonnet are called the octave.

Ode: A long lyric poem, serious in subject, elevated in style and elaborate in structure.

Onomatopoeia: The phenomenon of the sounds of a word reflecting the sense (*e.g.*, 'hiss'). Sometimes it is also used for sound symbolism.

Oxymoron: The figurative combination of seemingly contradictory elements (*e.g.* dark light).

Opacity: The phenomenon of the reference being not transparent. For example,
He wants to marry *the tallest girl.*
Here 'the tallest' might be referring to a particular tall girl or just a girl who is very tall.

Operative: This is a term in the system of sentential voice Halliday postulates for English, the other terms being 'middle' and 'receptive'. The operative and middle voice sentences will have an active verb whereas the receptive may have either an active verb or a passive verb. For example,
Operative: He is washing clothes.
Middle: He is snoring.

Receptive:
These clothes don't wash well.
These clothes have been washed.
These clothes have been washed by Mary.

Paradox: A statement which is seemingly absurd but valid when probed into thoroughly.

Parallelism: Correspondence between one unit and another. (see Coupling)

Paraphrase: A sentence is considered a paraphrase of another if the two have the 'same' meaning. Actually the sameness is in 'experiental' and 'rhetorical' (interactional) functional values. 'Synonymy' of the lexical items is comparable to paraphrasal relationship of sentences. Paraphrasally related sentences can also be called 'allosentences' (Verma) or 'agnate sentences' (Halliday).

Parataxis: The sequential relationship that obtains among elements with the functional value of 'coordination' or 'apposition'. Here if three elements are paratactically related there is 'transitive' relationship between non-adjacent elements. For example, 1 2 3 will be:
1–2
2–3
1–3
(– = sequentially following with a specific relationship).

Participants: The experiential roles like actor, beneficiary, goal, etc. These include all the roles that nominals play excepting those specifying time, place and manner.

Paryāya Śabda: Synonym.

Passivity: Where the subject is the sufferer of the process reflected in the verb we have passivity.

Paśyanti: The supreme reality, the flash of insight or the principle of consciousness. Here there is no distinction between speech and thought. This is the stage where sphoṭa obtains.

Patient: It refers to the entity which is in a certain state, or changes its state or is affected by the verb. For example,
She washed *clothes.*
Road is wide.

Pentameter: A line of 5 feet.

Perceptual Plausibility: This is the weaker sibling of 'psychological reality'; a linguist's description should accord with the native speaker's intuitions—at least it should not go violently against it; it should be plausible as far as the speaker's perception is concerned (Prakasam 1976b).

Performative: An expression, explicit or implicit, which tells us of the intention of the performer of the speech act. For example:
"*I warn you* not to do it."
"I warn you" is an explicit performative clause and 'warn' is the performative verb. But in
"Don't do it"
"I WARN you" is an implicit performative hypersentence.

Perlocution: The effects, planned or unplanned, created by a speech act by using a particular sentence. For example,
"He persuaded me to remain absent."

Periphrasis: A round-about way of naming some thing; the use of circumlocution.

Personification: Endowing things or abstractions with life or especially human traits.

Phenotype Language/Phenotype Grammar: Concrete natural language; grammar of natural language (Shauman).

Phonegment: The phonological segment (phoneme, phonematic unit) with its constituent feature distinguished for 'static' and 'dynamic' values (Prakasam and Sodhi 1992).

Poetic Diction: The choice of words used in a poem or in poetry.

Poetics: Theory or doctrine of poetry.

Polysemy: The multiplicity of meanings a given lexical item has (cf, homonymy). We might get genuine cases of indeterminacy between polysemy and homonymy.

Polysyndeton: The repetition of conjunctions.

Pragmatics: The study of the sociocultural and contextual condition that affect the appropriate use of languge in communication (cf. prakaraṇa).

Pragmatic Presuppositions: are connected with the relationship between a sentence and the context in which it is used. They are conditions necessary for a sentence to be appropriate in the context in which it is used.

Pragmeme: The minimal feature of the background against which language is used. This is the minimal feature of significance which is *not a constituent of a lexeme*. The minimal feature of significance which is a constituent of the lexeme is 'sememe'. The feature 'bovine' is a sememe and the feature 'sacred' is pragmeme with reference to 'cow' (Prakasam 1999: 111).

Prakaraṇa; Prakaraṇa Śastra: Context of situation; that which is not available in a sentence but necessary for getting the complete message of the sentence. It is present in the perception of the speaker-hearer. The study of 'prakaraṇa' can be taken as pragmatics (= Prakaraṇa śastra).

Pratyakṣa: Direct perception

Predication: This is a semantic unit which can be characterized as the 'complete thought' a clause expresses. Other terms used for this unit are 'assertion' and 'proposition'; this term may also be used to signify the process of 'predicating' *i.e.*, expressing an item as predicate of a subject.

Presupposition: The condition which is necessary for a sentence to be true or false (cf. Entailment, Implication).

Projection Rules: The rules that reconstruct the speaker's ability to project sentence-meanings from morpheme-meanings." These rules and the 'dictionary' of a language constitute its semantic component. The inputs are underlying phrase-markers and the outputs are semantic interpretations (Katz).

Prominence: Linguistic highlighting, which reflects semantic highlighting.

Proposition: The thought (or sense) of a sentence (simple sentence or clause) (cf. Predication). Proposition in the Fillmorian theory consists of a *verb* followed by a sequence of one or more nouns with specified casal relations.

Prose Rhythm: The rhythm of the casual language.

Prouḍhokti: Elevated expression.

Psychological Reality: 'Functional validity' of a given analysis (Chomsky); the claim that *an* analysis somehow reflects the way a speaker 'thinks' or 'feels' about his language. The underlying representation which is assumed to be in the 'mind' of the speaker-hearer is characterized by psychological reality.

Pun: A figurative use of a word in several senses.

Pyrhic: A foot of 2 unaccented syllables.

Rasa: Aesthetic emotion.

Rasika: The man of taste.

Receptive: The clause where the subject is not the actor but sufferer or goal of the process. This is generally accompanied by passive voice in the verb. 'Operative-receptive' distinction can be applicable also in equative clauses. For example,
Q. What did Mohan paint?
A. He painted the ship (operative).
Q. Who painted the ship?
A. The ship was painted by Mohan (receptive).
Q. What is Mohan?
A. He is the teacher (operative).
Q. Who is the teacher?
A. Mohan is the teacher (receptive).

Redundancy: The phenomenon of a given feature not being required in a descriptive analysis as it *is predictable* on the basis of another feature. For example, the feature 'concrete' is redundant while specifying the features for 'boy' because 'human' presupposes the feature 'concrete'.

Referent: The item referred to by an expression. We might get two expressions with the same referent but two different senses.

Register: The language variety along the dimension of subject matter. For example,
  Journalese
  Officialese
  Scientific register.

Relativism: The hypothesis that the language one speaks profoundly affects one's thought processes and the way one interprets the world. This relativistic view of the cognitive structure of languages is known by the name of the 'Sapir-Whorf hypothesis'.

Rhyme: A metrical device consisting of the sound identities of line-final positions.

Rhythm: The patterning of syllables of different quantities and qualities.

Rīti: The theory of arrangement of sound and sense for the purpose of producing poetic effect.

Rūḍha: Conventional.

Sahṛdaya: The critic/reader/spectator with a sympathetic heart.

Samatā: Parallelism (cf coupling).

Sādhya: Derived, achieved.

Sāhacharya: Mutual association. In samyoga and viprayoga we have an explicit expression signifying connection, e.g., 'with', 'without', but in sahacharya such an expression is absent.

Saṃnidhi: The condition that the words in a sentence should be contiguous in time (also known as 'āsatti); this contiguity is uninterrupted utterance' or 'unbroken apprehension of words'. This can be taken to be referring to the 'supra-segmental phonological markers' which bind words into a phrase or a clause. Some thinkers use 'saṃnidhi' to refer to semantic affinity between an utterance and the available referent, e.g., 'kilo of potatoes, please' lacks 'saṃnidhi' when said before a milk booth.

Saṃsarga (contact), **Samyoga** (association): The connection that is generally known to exist between two things—this is one of the contextual factors (cotextual) useful for disambiguating a polysemous expression. For example: *Bank with lockers.* Here 'lockers' refers to 'money bank', but not 'river bank'.

Sāmarthya: The capacity that is known from the effect; this helps us disambiguate a polysemous word. For example,
The *bank* did not honour my cheque.
Here 'honoring a cheque' is possible only for a 'money bank'.

Scansion: The system of metrical analysis graphically represented.

Scatter: The different grammatical forms of a given lexeme, e.g., kind, kindly, kindness, unkind (of 'kind').

Scope: The element or elements affected by a given category, e.g., the scope of negation.

Selectional Restriction: The condition under which the sense represented by a set of semantic markers can combine with other senses to form the sense of a syntactic complex constituent (Katz).

Semantic Syntax: See Generative Semantics.

Semantics and Pragmatics: Semantics is the study of code-based signification and pragmatics is the study of coder-based significantion.

Seme: The minimal feature of meaning.

Sememe: The minimal feature of lexical meaning, whereas 'pragmeme' is the minimal feature of contextual meaning.

Sense: One of the discrete meanings of a word; it should be distinguished from 'reference'.

Sestet: The last 6 lines of a sonnet.

Set: The open set of lexical items; the set of paradigmatically related lexical items; *e.g.* good, nice, kind.

Setting Selection: Seeks to account for the way in which the different aspects of the socio-physical world control the understanding sentences.

Siddha: Inherent, innate.

Siddhapada Sānnidhya: The syntactic connection with word already known; the grammatical 'value' leading to deciphering content.

Sign: The (linguistic) sign is the inseparable two-faced item, the two faces being the 'signifier' and the 'signified'.

Significance: The 'meaning' of phonological or graphological elements.

Signification: Meaning (content) of a sign.

Silent Ictus: The stressed position which does not get any syllabic realization.

Simile: The figurative comparison of one thing with another using a specific term as vehicle of comparison.

Situation: The extralinguistic context of situation (cf. Hjelmslev content-substance).

Sociolect: The language variety differentiated on the dimension of social background or status of the speaker(s).

Source: The starting point of the movement of an object in the case of the movement verbs and is the starting state of the object whic undergoes the change of the state verbs.

Span: The collocational span; the co-occurrence capabilities of given lexeme. For example:
strong tea, strong argument
powerful argument
* powerful tea.

Speech-act: A linguistic act in a communicative situation.

Sphoṭa: An integral unit, an individual, language-symbol conveying meaning.

Style: The language variety differentiated on the dimension of formality.

Spondee: A foot consisting of 2 accented syllables.

Stress: The emphasis received by a syllable as part of a metrical pattern; the inherent strength of a syllable (see accent).

Stress Maximum: Stress placed between two unstressed positions.

Style: The characteristic way in which a literary piece is structurated. It encompasses everything that concerns the use of language and its signification in literature.

Stylistics: The study of style. It involves the categories of phonology and prosody, morphology and syntax, semantics and pragmatics, and lexicology to arrive at a comprehensive study of the expression as the manifesting counterpart of meaning.

Subordination/Superordination: See Hyponymy.

Substance: The phonic/graphic substance (cf. Hjelmslev, expression-substance).

Summative Word: A word in a poem which is (i) semantically important (ii) phonologically important and (iii) positionally important.

Surface Structure: The morphosyntactic structure of an expression which is off deep structure and oriented towards phonologic structure.

Svabhāvokti: The least affected poetic expression; natural expression (but not common place).

Syllable: The smallest measurable unit of speech. It is the prime of metre, mainly identified as accented or unaccented syllable.

Symbol: The manner of using an object or idea to signify something else by way of association or suggestion.

Symbolization: is a process by which post-semantic units of a surface representation are replaced by underlying phonologic configuration.

Synaloepha: Contraction or omission of vowels.

Syncope: Omission of a sound from the middle of a word.

Synonymy: The phenomenon of several words having the same meaning.

Syntheticity: The phenomenon of a given sentence depending on an actual situation for its truth value. The sentence
Teachers are honest men
requires empirical evidence for it to be true.

System: The paradigmatically related (grammatical or semantic or phonological) categories constituting a 'closed' (finite) system, e.g.,
the system of tense
the system of gender
the system of pronouns.

Tātparya: The intention of the speaker or the general purport of a sentence.

Tautology: The phenomenon of invariability of truth. For example, *that spinster is not married* is invariably true, and so tautological.

Tension: Clash between two different aspects of expression or content; 'counterpoint' is metrical tension.

Thematic: Concerning the topical values of different part of a structure.

Thematization or Topicalization: Initializing an element where it is not to occur in an unmarked sentence.

Theme: (i) Topic is part of "Topic-comment" structure. Theme is part of theme-rheme structure. Theme is the point of departure for a given sentence (or clause). (ii) The subject matter of a literary piece.

Thesis: The specific meaning of a given text; the semantic interpretation of a text.

Thesis Rhythm: The rhythm effected by the semantic structure of a verse line.

Tenor: The meaning of a metaphor.

Textual: The function of language which refers to the organization of texts.

Tone: The pitch movement we notice in an utterance.

Tone Group: The part of utterance which is marked by a single pitch-movement (complex ones are also to be considered single tones).

Tonic Element: That part of the tonegroup which carries the tonic.

Tonic Stress: The Nuclear stress (or sentence stress) whence the pitch takes off. The word or phrase bearing this stress is the most important bit of information.

Topic: The word or phrase about which the rest of the sentence says something.

Transfer Feature: A feature transferred from one item to another. In "I like *Shakespeare*" Shakespeare is to be taken as the plays of Shakespeare.

Trochee: A foot with an accented syllable followed by an unaccented syllable.

Uddeśya: The 'given' element, known to both the encoder and the decoder.

Unity: One of the most important principles of verbal arts. It refers to the well cohered beginning, middle and end of a literary piece. It also refers to the coherence of different parts of a given text.

Universe: The subject (matter) chosen by the poet to be talked about in his poem (primary universe). Thesis is the secondary universe.

Upamāna: Identification of an object from known description.

Upapatti: Arguments in favour of the main topic which need to be considered to get at the message (taçtparya) of a passage.

Vaikhari: The actual sounds uttered by the speaker and heard by the listener.

Vakrokti: The specilized or peculiar expression of a poem; the deviation is from the day to day language.

Vākyaśeṣa: The rest of the passage in the context (cotext).

Valence: See Ākāṅkṣā.

Valency: A valency grammar presents a model of sentence containing a fundamental element (the verb) and a number of dependent elements whose type is determined by the 'valency' attributed to the verb. The term was introduced by the French linguist Lucien Tesniere (1893-1954).

Value: The meaning of a lexico-grammatical item; the value of a poem is the aesthetic emotion it nurtures in the heart of a reader.

Vehicle: The vehicle of metaphor.

Vidheya: The 'New' element, known only to the encoder, or is chosen to highlight.

Vikalpa: The mental construct of the image.

Viprayoga: The disappearance of the connection that is known to exist between two things, *e.g., Bank without lockers.*

Vivakshā: Intention of a speaker.

Virodhitā: Opposition or hostility or contrast:
"*man* and god" (human being)
'*man* and woman' (adult, male, human being).

Vivṛiti: Explanation, commentary.

Vṛtti: 'Function of a word'; speed of utterance.

Vṛddhavyavahāra: The usage of words by elders; this is one of the ways we learn meanings of words (lexical content).

Vyakti: The particular (token); grammatical gender.

Bibliography

Abbi, A., 1975, 1980. *Reduplication in Hindi: A Generative Semantic Study*. Ph.D. diss. Cornell University. A much revised version is published under the title *Semantic Grammar of Hindi: A Study of Reduplication*. New Delhi: Bahri Publications.

Abercrombie, D., 1964. *"A Phonetician's view of verse structure"* Linguistics VI: 5-13.

Abercrombie, D., 1967. *Elements of General Phonetics*. Edinburgh University Press.

Anderson, J.H., 1971. *The Grammar of Case—Towards a Localist Theory*. *Cambridge*: Cambridge University Press.

Antal, L., 1964. *Content, Meaning and Understanding*. The Hague: Mouton.

Ardener, E. (ed.), 1971. *Social Anthropology and Language*. A.S.A. Monograph 10. Tavistock Publications.

Bach, E. and R.J. Harms (ed.), 1968. *Universals in Linguistic Theory*. New York: Holt, Rinehart and Winston.

Bach, E., 1968. 'Nouns and Noun Phrases' in Bach & Harms (eds.) *Universals in Linguistic Theory*. New York: Holt, Rinehart and Winston.

Bailey, C.J.N. and R. Shuy (eds.), 1973. *New Ways in Analysing Variation in English*. Washington D.C.: Georgetown University Press.

Bartsch, R. and T. Vennemann, 1972. *Semantic Structures*. Frankfurt: Athenaum.

Bates, E., 1976. *Language and Context—The Acquisition of Pragmatics*. New York: Academic Press.

Bateson, F.W., 1971. "Literature and Linguistics: A reply" in Fowler (1971): 54-64.

Bazell, C.E. *et al*. (eds.) 1966. *In Memory of J.R. Firth*. London: Longman.

Beaver, J.C., 1970. "A Grammar of Prosody " in Reeman (ed.) (1970): 442-447.

Bhattacharya, B., 1962. *A Study in Language and Meaning*. Calcutta: Progressive Publishers.

Birch, D. and Michael *Functions of Style* London: Printer O'Toole (ed) 1988 Publishers.

Bloomfield, L., 1933. *Language*. New York: Holt, Rinehart and Winston.

Brazil, D., 1975. *Discourse Intonation*. English Language Research: Birmingham University.

Brooks, C., 1960. "The language of Paradox" in Tate (ed.) (1960): 37-61.
Brough, J., 1951. 'Theories of General Linguistics in Sanskrit Grammarians' in *Transactions of the Philological Society*, 27-46.
Brough, J., 1953. 'Some Indian Theories of Meaning' in *Transactions of the Philological Society*, 161-76.
Buhler, K., 1934. *Sprach Theorie*. Jena Fischer.
Bursill-Hall, G.L., 1971. *Speculative Grammars of the Middle Ages*. The Hague: Mouton.
Burton, D.L., and J.S. Simmons (eds.). *Teaching English in Today's High Schools*. New York: Holt, Rinehart and Winston.
Caffarel, A., J.R. Martin and Christian M.I.M. Matthiessen 2004. *Language Typology a Functional Perspective*. Amsterdam: John Benjamins Publishing Company.
Chafe, W., 1970. *Meaning and the Structure of Language*. Chicago: The University of Chicago Press.
Chafe, W., 1972. 'Discourse Structure and Human Knowledge' in *Language Comprehension and the Acquisition of Knowledge*, ed. by. Roy O. Frudle and John B. Cornell. Washington: V. H. Winston.
Chafe, Wallace., 1974. 'Language and Consciousness' in Language, 50, 111-33.
Chafe, Wallace L., 1976. 'Givenness, Contrastiveness, Definiteness, Subjects, Topics and Point of View' in *Subject and Topic*. N.L. Charles (ed.). New York: Academic Press.
Chari, V.K., 1976. "Poetic emotions and Poetic semantics" in *The Journal of Aesthetics and Art Criticism* (IV I No. 3:287-300).
Chatman, S., 1960. "Comparing metrical styles" in Sebeok (ed) (1960): 149-172.
Chatman, S., 1970 "The components of English metre" in Freemen (ed.) (1970): 309-35.
Chomsky, N., 1957. *Syntactic Structures*. The Hague: Mouton.
Chomsky, N., 1965. *Aspects of the Theory of Syntax*. Cambridge, Massachusetts: M.I.T. Press.
Chomsky N., 1971. *'Deep Structure, Surface Structure, and Semantic Interpretation'* in Semantics ed. by D.D. Steinberg and L.A. Jakoboyits, 1971, 119-207.
Chomsky, N., 1975. *Reflections on Language*. New York: Pantheon Books.
Chomsky, N., 1977. *Essays on Form and Interpretation*. New York: North-Holland.

Chomsky, N. and Howard Lasnik, 1977. 'Filters and Control', *Linguistic Inquiry,* Vol. 8, 425-504.
Chomsky, N., 1980. 'On Binding', *Linguistic Inquiry,* Vol. 11, 1–46.
Chomsky, N., 1981. *Lectures on Government and Binding.* Dordrecht-Holland: Foris Publications.
Chomsky, N., 1983. *Some Concepts and Consequences of the Theory of Government and Binding.* Cambridge, Massachusetts: M.I.T. Press.
1986 *Knowledge of language: Its nature origin and Use* New York: Praeger.
1995 *The Minimalist Paradigm* Cambridge MA; MIT press.
Chomsky, N., 200 *New Horizons in the Study of Language and Mind.* Cambridge: Cambridge University Press.
Cole, P., 1978. 'On the Origins of Referential Opacity' in Cole P. (ed.) 1978: 1-22.
Cole, P. (ed.), 1978. *Syntax and Semantics: Pragmatics,* Vol. 9. New York: Academic Press.
Cole, P. (ed.), 1981. *Radical Pragmatics.* New York: Academic Press.
Cole, P. and Morgan (eds.), 1975. *Syntax and Semantics*: Speech Acts, Vol. 3. New York: Academic Press.
Cook, W.A., 1972 (a). 'A Set of Postulates of Case Grammar Analysis' in *Working Papers in Languages and Linguistics,* No. 4, 35-49 Washington D.C.: Georgetown University Press.
Cook, W.A., 1972 b). 'A Case Grammar Matrix', *Working Papers in Languages and Linguistics,* No. 6, 15-45. Washington D.C.: Georgetown University Press.
Crane, R.S. 1953. *The Language of criticism and the structure of poetry.* University of Toronto Press.
De, S.K. (ed), (1961) *The Vakrokti Jivata* Calcutta: Firma K.L. Mukhopadhyaya, Third revised edition (First-Edn. 1923).
De, S.K. (ed), 1960. *Sanskrit Poetics* (in 2 volumes) Calcutta.
Dillon, G. I., 1977. *Introduction to Contemporary Linguistic Semantics.* Englewood Cliffs: Prentice Hall Inc.
Dinneen, F.P., 1968. *An Introduction to General Linguistics.* New York: Holt, Rinehart and Winston.
Dixon, R.M.W., 1964.'On Formal and Contextual Meaning', *Acta Linguistica.*
Dorsch, T.S. (ed), 1965 *Classical Literary Criticism* Harmondsworth: Penguin Books.
Ellis, J., 1976 'On Contextual Meaning' in Bazell *et al.* (1966), 79-95.

Emonds, J., 1976. *Transformational Approach to English Syntax*. New York: Academic Press.
Empson, W., 1953. *Seven Types of Ambiguity*. London: Chatto and Windus (3rd Edition).
Feigi, H., Sellars W., and Lehrer K., (eds.), 1972. *New Readings in Philosophical Analysis*. New York: Appleton Century–Crofts.
Fillmore, C.J., 1967. 'Grammar of Hitting and Breaking' in *Working Papers in Linguistics*, 1. The Ohio State University.
Fillmore, C.J., 1968. 'The Case For Case' in Universals in Linguistic Theory. E. Bach and R.T. Harms (ed.). New York: Holt, Rinehart and Winston.
Fillmore, C.J., 1970. 'Subjects, Speakers and Roles', *Working Papers in Linguistics*, No. 4, Ohio State University.
Fillmore, C.J., 1971(a). 'Some problems for Case Grammar, Monograph series on Languages and Linguistics, No. 24. Washington D.C.: Georgetown University Press.
Fillmore, C.J., 1971(b). 'Types of Lexical Information', *Semantics: An Interdisciplinary Reader in Philosophy, Linguistics and Psychology*, (ed.) D.D. Steinberg and L.A. jakobovits, 370-92.
Fillmore, C.J., 1971(c). 'Verbs of Judging: An Exercise in Semantic Description' in *Studies in Linguistic Semantics*, ed. by C.J. Fillmore and D. Langndoen, 273-90.
Firth, J.R., 1951. "Modes of Meaning" reprinted in *Papers in Linguistics 1934-1951*. (1957, O.U.P.,) PP 190-215.
Firth, J.R., 1935. 'The Technique of Semantics', reprinted in Firth, 1957, 7-33.
Firth, J.R., 1957. Papers in Linguistics 1934-51. London: O.U.P.
Fodor, J.A. and J.J. Katz (eds.), 1963. *The Structure of Language: Readings in the Philosophy of Language*. Englewood Cliffs, New Jersey: Prentice-Hall Inc.
Fodor, J.A., 1977. *Semantics: Theories of Meaning in Generative Grammar*. New York: Harper and Row.
Fowler, R. (ed) 1966. *Essays on Style and Language* London: Routedge and Kegan Paul.
Fowler, R., 1971. *The Language of Literature* London: Routiedge and Kegan Paul.
Fowler, R., 1975. *Style and Structure in Literature* London: Blackwell.
Frege, G., 1892. 'Uber Sinn and Bedeutung', Zeitschrift fur Philosophic and Philosophische Kritik, 100, 25-50. Translated as *On Sense and Nominatum*, in Feigl and Sellars (eds.), 1972.

Freeman, D.(ed), 1970. *Linguistics and Literary Style*. New York: Holt, Rinehart and Winston Inc.

Fudge, E., 1970. "Phonological structure and "expressiveness" *Journal of Linguistics*. 6:22-61.

Fujimura, 0. (ed.), 1973. *Three Dimensions of Linguistic Theory*-Tokyo: TEC Co.

Gardiner, A.H., 1951. The Theory of Speech and Language. London: O.U.P.

Gazdar, G., 1979. *Pragmatics*. New York: Academic Press.

Givon, T., 1978. 'Negation in Language: Pragmatics, Function, Ontology' in Cole (ed.) 1978: 69-112.

Givon, T. (ed.), 1979. *Discourse and Syntax*. New York: Academic Press.

Grice, H.P., 1978. 'Further Notes on Logic and Conversation' in Cole (ed.) 19.21 113-27.

Grice, H.P., 1981. 'Presupposition and Conversational Implicature' in Cole, P. (ed.), *Radical Pragmatics*, New York: Academic Press. 183-98.

Gross, Maurice, 1979. 'On the Failure of Generative Grammars', Language, Vol. 55, 859-85.

Hass, W., 1954. 'On defining Linguistic Units', Transactions of the Philological Society, 54-84.

Halle, M. and "Chaucer and the study of prosody" in Freeman Keyser, S.J. 1970 (ed), 366-426.

Halliday, M.A.K., 1957. 'Some Aspects of Systematic Description and Comparison in Grammatical Analysis' in Studies in Linguistic Analysis. Oxford: Blackwell.

Halliday, M.A.K., 1961. 'Categories of the Theory of Grammar', Word, 18: 54-72.

Halliday, M.A.K., 1966. 'Lexis as a Linguistic Level', in Bazell *et al.* (ed.), 1966: 148-62.

Halliday, M.A.K. and A. MCINTOSH, 1966. Patterns of Language. London: Longman.

Halliday, M.A.K., 1967-68. 'Notes on Transitivity and Theme in 'English', Journal of Linguistics, Vol. 3 (1967), 37-81, 199-244; Vol. 4 (1968), 179-215.

Halliday, M.A.K., 1967(a). *Intonation and Grammar in British English*. The Hague: Mouton.

Halliday, M. A. K., 1967(b). *Some Aspects of the Thematic Organization of the English Clause*. Santa Monica: The Rand Corporation.

Halliday, M.A.K., 1970a. "Functional diversity in language etc" *Foundations of language* 6:322-61.

Halliday, M.A.K., 1970b. A Course in Spoken English London: O.U.P.
Halliday, M.A.K., 1970c. "Descriptive Linguistics in Literary studies" in Freeman ed (1970): 57-72.
Halliday, M.A.K., 1973a. Explorations in the functions of language London: Edward Arnold.
Halliday, M.A.K., and R. Hasan, 1976. *Cohesion in English* London: Longman.
Halliday, M. A. K., 1973b. *Learning How to Mean: Explorations in the Development of Language.* London: Edward Arnold.
Halliday, M.A.K., 1976. *Language as Social Semiotic.* London: Edward Arnold.
Halliday, M.A.K. 2002. *Collected Works of M.A.K. Halliday* Vol. 1 (ed.) Jonathan Webster London: Continuum.
Halliday, M.A.K., 2014. *Halliday's Introduction to Functional Grammar* (Revised by Christian M.I.M. Matthiessen). London: Routledge.
Harman, G. and Davidson, 1972. *Semantics for Natural Language.* Dordrecht: C.U.P.
Haspelmath, M. 2006. "Against markedness (and what to replace it with)". *Journal of Linguistics* 42:25-70.
Hjelmslev, L. 1953, Prolegomena to a Theory of Language trans by F.J. whitefield. Bloanifton: Indiana University Press.
Hymes, D. 1960. "Closing statement: Linguistics and poetics" in Sebeok (ed). 109-31.
Jackendoff, R.S., 1972. *Semantic Interpretation in Generative Grammar.* Cambridge, Massachusetts: MIT Press.
Jakobson, R., 1960. "Closing statement: Linguistics and Poetics" In Sebeok (ed). 1960: 350-77.
Katz, J.J., 1966. *The Philosophy of Language.* New York: Harper & Row.
Katz, J.J., 1971. 'Interpretive Semantics vs. Generative Semantics', Foundations of Language, 6, 220-29.
Katz, J.J., 1972. *Semantic Theory.* New York: Harper and Row.
Katz, J.J., T.G. Bever and D.T. Langedoen (eds.), 1976. *An Integrated Theory of Linguistic Ability. New York: Crowell.*
Katz, J.J. and J.A. Fodor, 1963. 'The Structure of a Semantic Theory', Language, 39: 2, 170-210.
Katz, J.J. and P.M. Postal, 1964. *An Integrated Theory of Linguistic Descriptions.* Cambridge, Massachusetts: M.I.T. Press.
Katz, J.J., 1980. 'Chomsky on Meaning', Language, 56: 1, 1-41.
Katz J.J., 1981. *Language and Other Abstract Objects.* Oxford: Blackwell.
Kelkar, A.R., 1969. "The Being of a poem" *Foundations of Language* 5:17-33.

Keenan, E.L. (ed.), 1975. *Formal Semantics of Natural Language.* New York: C.U.P.

Kempson, R., 1975. *Presupposition and the Delimitation of Semantics.* Cambridge: C.U.P.

Kempson, R., 1977. *Semantic Theory.* Cambridge: C.U.P.

Kiefer, F. (ed.), 1969. *Studies in Syntax and Semantics.* Dordrecht: Reidel.

Kress, G. (ed.), 1975. *Halliday: System and Function in Language.* London: O.U.P.

Krishnachaitanya, 1965. *Sanskrit Poetics* Bombay: Asia Publishing House.

Krishnamurthi, K., 1974. *Anandavardhana's Dhvanyaloka* Dharwar: Karnataka University.

Krishnamurthy, N. Sunita Mishra and R.V. Ram 2013; *India's Language Philodophy* Delhi; Pearson.

Korg. J, 1959. *An Introduction to Poetry* New York: Holt, Rinehart & Winston.

Kunjunni, Raja K., 1963. *Indian Theories of Meaning.* Madras: The Adyar Library and Research Centre.

Kuroda, S.Y., 1971. 'Two Remarks on Pronominalization', Foundations of Language, 7, 331-51.

Kuppuswami, Sastry, 1945. *Highways and Byways of Literary criticism.*

Lado, R. *Linguistics Across Cultures.*

La Galy, M., R. Fox and A. Bruck (eds.), 1974. *Papers from the Tenth Regional Meeting of the Chicago Linguistic Society.* Chicago, Illinois: University of Chicago.

Lakoff, G., 1965. *On the Nature of Syntactic Irregularity.* Ph.D., diss. Indiana. The revised version published under the title *Irregularity in Syntax*, 1970. New York: Holt, Rinehart and Winston.

Lakoff, G., 1971. 'On Generative Semantics' in Steinberg and Jakobovits (eds.), *Semantics: An Interdisciplinary Reader in Philosophy, Linguistics and Psychology.* London, New Yoylc: Cambridge University Press, 232-96.

Lakoff, G., 1972. 'Hedges: A Study in Meaning Criteria and the Logic of Fuzzy Concepts' in Paranteav, Levi and Pharas (eds.) *Papers from the Eighth Regional Meeting of the Chicago Liguistic Society.* Chicago: University of Chicago.

Lakoff, G., 1973. 'The Inseparability of Semantics and Pragmatics' paper presented at the Texas Conference of Performatives, Conversational Implicatures and Presuppositions. Austin: Texas.

Lakoff, G., 1974. Interview with Herman Parret. In Fillmore, G. Lakoff, and R. Lakoff, (eds.)
Lakoff, G., 1975. 'Pragmatics in natural logic' in Keenan (1975): 253-56.
Lee, I.J., 1941. *Language Habits in Human Affairs.* New York: Harper and Row.
Leech, G.N., 1966. "Linguistics and the figures rhetoric" in Fowler (ed) (1966) 135-56.
Leech, G.N., 1967. *English in Advertising.* London: Longman.
Leech, G.N., 1970. The Bread I Break' - Language and Interpretation" in Freeman (ed) (1970): 40-56.
Leech, G.N., 1974. *Semantics.* Harmondsworth: Penguin.
Leech, G.N., 1983. *Principles of Pragmatics.* London: Longman.
Lyons, J. (ed.), 1970. *New Horizons in Linguistics.* Harmondsworth: Penguin Books.
Lyons, J., 1977. *Semantics* (in 2 volumes). Cambridge: C.U.P.
Maclay, H., 1971. 'Overview' in *Semantics: An Interdisciplinary Reader in Philosophy,* Linguistics and Psychology, eds. D.D. Steinberg and L.A. Jakobovits, 157-82.
Mccawley, J.D., 1973. *Grammar and Meaning.* Tokyo: Taishukan.
Mccawley, J.D. (ed.), 1976. *Syntax and Semantics: Notes from the Linguistic Underground,* Vol. 7. New York: Academic Press.
Mccawley, J.D., 1968. The Role of Semantics in a Grammar' in Bach and Harms (ed.), 1968: *Universals in Linguistic Theory,* ed. by Bach and Harms, 1970. England.
Mccawley, J.D., 1970. 'English as a VSO Language', Language, 46, 280-99.
Mccawley, J.D., 1971(a). 'Prelexical Syntax', Monograph series on Languages and Linguistics, No. 24. Georgetown University.
Mccawley, J.D., 1971(b). 'Tense and Time Reference in English' in Filmore and Langendoen (eds.), *Studies in Linguistic Semantics.*
'Morgan, J.L., 1978. 'Two Types of Convention in Indirect Speech Acts' in Cole (ed.) 1978, 261-80.
Newmeyer, Fredrick J., 1980. *Linguistic Theory in America: The First Quarter Century of Generative Grammar.* New York: Academic Press.
Newmeyer, Fredrick J., 1983. *Grammatical Theory.* Chicago: The University of Chicago Press.
Nida, E.A., 1957. *Learning a Foreign Language.* AnnArbor: Michigan University Press.
Nida, E.A., 1975. *Componential Analysis of Meaning.* The Hague: Mouton.

Ogden, C.K. and I.A. Richards, 1956. *The Meaning of Meaning.* Routledge and Kegan.

Osgood, C.E. et al., 1957. The Measurement of Meaning. University of Illinois Press.

O'Toole, L.M., 1974. "Functions of Language and the teaching of Literature" to appear in the proceedings of the Bauff International Congress of Slavists, Sept. 1974.

O'Toole, L.M., 1975. "Analytic and Synthetic approaches to narrative structure etc." in Fowler, (ed) (1975): 143-76.

O'Toole, L.M., 1976. "Narrative structure and Living Texture: Joyce's Two Gallants" PTL 3.1-21.

Pandeya, R.C., 1963. *The Problem of Meaning in Indian Philosophy.* Delhi: Motilal Banarsidas.

Parenteau, P.M., J.N. Levi and G.C. Phares (eds.), 1972. Papers from the Eighth Regional Meeting of the Chicago Linguistic Society. Chicago, Illinois: Chicago Linguistic Society.

Perlmutter, D. and P. Postal, 1983. *Relational Grammar.* Chicago: The University of Chicago Press.

Parret Herman, 1974. *Discussing Language.* The Hague: Mouton.

Postal, P.M., 1974. *On Raising: One Rule of English Grammar and its Theoretical Implications.* Cambridge, Massachusetts: M.I.T. Press.

Prakasam, V., 1970. *The Syntactic Patterns of Telugu and English: A Study in Contrastive Analysis.* Hyderabad: CIEFL.

Prakasam V., 1976a. 'Functional Value of Phonological Features' in Acta Linguistica Hungaricae, 26, 77-88.

Prakasam. V., 1976b. "Perceptual Plausibility and a Language Game" Anthopological Linguistics. PP. 323-327.

Prakasam. V., 1979. 'Aspects of Sentence Phonology' in Archivurn-, Linguisticum, Vol. X (New series).

Prakasam, V., 1981. 'Aspects of Word Phonology', in New Developments in Systemic Linguistics. Halliday, M.A.K. and Fawcett, R. (eds.), London: Batesford.

Prakasam, V., 1982. *Functional Stylistics.* Patiala: Indian Institute of Language Studies.

Prakasam, V., 1985. *The Linguistic Spectrum* Patiala: Punjabi University.

Prakasam, V., 1986. "Sememe, pragmeme and the threshold" in (ed) O.N. Koul: *Language, Literature and Discourse,* New Delhi: Balaji Publications.

Prakasam, V., and Harinder Sodhi 1992. "Phonegment and Sandhi" in *Sound patterns for the Phonetician* (eds). T. Balasubramanian and V. Prakasam, Madras: T.R. Publications.
Prakasam, V., 1999. *Semiotics of Language, Literature and Culture.* New Delhi: Allied Publishers Pvt. Ltd.
Prakasam, V., 2004. "Towards a theory of pragmeme" (1981-95) in *Language, Context and Culture* (eds). Ashok Kumar, Lucknow: Gurukul Pulications.
Rahavan, V., 1973. *Studies on some concepts of the Alamkara Sastra* Madras: The Adyar Library and Research Centre, Revised Edition (First Edn. 1942).
Rieux, J. and Rothine, B.E. (ed.) 1975. *The Port Royal Grammar.* The Hague: Mouton.
Rollin, B.E. (ed.), 1975. The Port Royal Grammar, The Hague: Mouton.
Rivers, W., 1965. *The Psychologist and the Foreign Language Teacher.* Chicago: The University of Chicago Press.
Rommetveit, R., 1974. *On Message Structure.* New York, Wiley.
Ross, J.R., 1972. 'The Category Squish: Endstation Hauptwort 4, in, Peranteau, Levi and Phares, (eds.)
Ross, J.R., 1973(a). 'A Fake NP Squish' in Bailey and Shuy, (eds.).
Ross, J.R., 1973(b). 'Nouniness' in Fujimura, (ed.)
Ross, J.R., 1974. 'There, there, (there, (there, (there, . . .)))' in La Gaily, Fox and Bruck, eds.
Ross, J.R., 1975. 'Clause—mateness' in Keenan (ed.).
Saddock, J., 1974. *Towards a Linguistic Theory of Speech Acts.* New York: Seminar Press.
Sadighi, F. and Bavali, M. (2008) "Chomsky's Universal Grammar and Halliday's Systematic Functional Linguistics: An Appraisal and a Compromise". *Journal of Pan-Pacific Association of Applied Linguistics*, 12(1): 11-28.
Sankaran, A., 1929. *The Theories of Rasa and Dhvani.* Madras: The Adyar Library and Research Centre.
Searle, J.R., 1969. *Speech Acts.* Cambridge: O.U.P.
Seuren, P. (ed.), 1971. *Semantic Syntax.* London: O.U.P.
Sebeok T.A. (Ed)., *Style in Language*, New York: MIT and John Wiley 1960 and Sons Inc.
Shauffer, D.A., 1951. *The Selected Poetry and Prose of S.T. Coleridge* New York: The Modern Library.
Sharma, D., 1969. *The Differentiation Theory of Meaning in Indian Logic.* The Hague: Mouton.

Shaumyan, S., 1977. *Applicational Grammar as a Semantic Theory of Natural Language.* Edinburgh University Press.

Sinclair, J. Mal., 1966. 'Beginning the Study of Lexis' in Bazell et al. (eds.), 1966: 410-30.

Sitapati. G., 1936. "Accent in Telugu speech and Verse" *Indian Linguistics* 6 also IL Reprint Vol II (1965): 201-24.

Staal, J.F., and P. Kiparsky, 1968. 'Syntactic and Semantic Relations in Panini', Foundations of Language, 5, 83-117.

Steinberg D.D. and L.A. Jakobovits, 1971. *Semantics: An Interdisciplinary Reader in Philosophy Linguistics and Psychology.* Cambridge University Press.

Tarski, A., 1956. *Logic, Semantics, Metamathematics.* London: Oxford University Press.

Tate, A (ed.) 1960. *The Language of Poetry.* New York: Russel and Russel (First Published 1942).

Thompson, J. 1970. Linguistic structure and the poetic line" in Freeman (ed) 1970): 36-46.

Verma, S.K., 1967. *An introduction to Systemic Grammar.* (Mimeo: C1EFL).

Verna, S.K., 1968-69. 'Allosentence: A Study in "Universals"' in *Linguistic Theory.* CIE Bulletin 7: 29-40.

Verma S.K. 1976: "Topicalization as stylistic mechanism" in Poetics (March, 1976): 23-33.

Vennemann, T., 1975. 'Topics, Sentence accent, Ellipsis: a proposal for their formal treatment' in Keenan (1975): 313-28.

Walpole, H.R., 1941. *Semantics: The Nature of Words and their Meanings.* W. W. Norton & Co.

Weinreich, U., 1966. 'Explorations in Semantic Theory' in Sebeok, T.A., (ed.), Current Trends in Linguistics, Vol. 3. The Hague: Mouton.

Wilks, Y., 1975. 'Preference Semantics' in Keenan (ed.), 1975.

Williams, Edwin, 1984. 'Lectures on Government and Binding', Review Article in *Language*, Vol. 60, No. 2, 400-4.

Wellek, R., (1976), "Closing statement" Sebeok (ed) (1960): 408-19.

Wellek, R. and Warren, A. 1963. *Theory of Literature Harmondsworth:* Penguin Books (3rd Edition: First published 1949).

Widdowson, H.G., 1975. Stylistics and the teaching of literature London: Longman.

Wilde, O, 1921. Interactions London: Methuen and Co. Ltd. XIV Edition (first published 1891).

ZIFF, P., 1960. *Semantic Analysis.* Ithaca: Cornell University Press.

Index

Abbi, A., 41, 191
Abercrombie, D., 116, 120, 135, 191
Abhihitānvaya vāda, 14, 20, 161
Abstractions, 157, 161
Ākānkṣā, 61, 161
Ānandavardhana, 5
Action process verbs, 42-47
Action Verbs, 42-47
Action, 161
Actives, 60, 61
Adhyāhāra, 10, 161
Akhaṇḍapakṣā, 3, 161
Ambient Verbs, 48
Ambiguity, 64, 112, 154-155, 162
Analogists, 162
Analyticity, 162
Anapaest, 135, 136, 162
Anderson, J.H., 165
Anekaśabda Darśana, 10, 162
Anomalists, 162
Anomaly, 162
Antal, L., 90
Antonymy, 163
Anvitābhidānavāda, 14, 163
Apoha theory, 6, 7, 163
Apūrvata, 163
Ardener, E., 191
Argument, 163
Asatti, 9, 184
Assertion, 56, 163-164
Auchitya, 101, 102, 164
Autonomous syntax, 26, 164

Bach, E., 191
Bacon, Roger, 15
Bailey, C.J.N, 191
Bartsh, R, 26, 39
Bates, E., 69-70
Bavali, 63
Bazell, C.E., 191
Beaver, 117, 138

Beneficiary, 164
Bever, T.G., 196
Bhāmaha, 98
Bhartṛhari, 5, 8, 10
Bhattacharya, B., 191
Bloomfield, L., 153,
Bounding theory, 63
Brazil, D., 78, 191
Brooks, 102
Brough, J., 3, 8, 9, 192
Buhler, K., 201
Bursill-Hall, G.L., 192
Burton, D.L., 192

Case categories, 51-52
Case grammar, 165
Causative verb, 165
Caesura, 117, 136, 165
Chafe, 11, 38-50, 173, 176
Chari, 99
Chatman, 117
Chomsky, N., 57-64
Christabel, 116
Circumstantials, 121, 167
Clusters, 24, 165
Clustering, 111, 133, 166
Cohesion, 110-11, 130-131
Cole, P., 72-73
Coleridge, 116
Colligation, 111, 133, 166
Collocation, 78, 87-88, 111, 133, 146-147, 167, 186
Communicative, 167
Competence, 167
Complement, 167
 nouns, 48
Completable verbs, 48
Configurations, 24, 167
Connotation, 159, 167
Connotative predicates, 56, 167

Constative utterance, 167
Construct grammar, 167
Constructing phenotype
  grammar, 65-67
Construction, types of, 24-5
Content, 89-90, 148-149, 169
Context, 77-91, 148-149, 169
Contextual factors, 12-14
Contextual translation, 152
Contradictory sentence, 169
Control theory, 63
Conventional implicatures, 75
Conversational implicature, 76, 168
Conversational postulates, 70
Cook, W.A., 43-47
Cooperative principle, 168, 175
Coordinate bilinguals, 168
Coupling, 103, 112-114, 131, 169
Counterpoint, 115, 169
Crane, 106
Cultural patterns, 158

De, 103-105, 113
Deep structure, 30-31, 53, 58-60, 169
Deep word-form, 169
Deixis system, 169
Delimination construction, 25
Demi-levels, 79-83
Denotation, 159, 169
Derivation process, 42-43
Derivational units, 39
Deviance, 102, 103
Dhvani theory, 99-100
Dhvani, 102, 169
Dialect, 82, 169
Diaresis, 117, 169
Dixon, R.M.W, 78, 86, 89-91
Dorsch, 101, 104-105

Effability, 22, 170
Ekaśabda darśana, 10, 170
Ellipsis, 170
Ellis, J., 78, 81-82, 85-86, 89-90

Emotive, 159, 170
Empson, W., 154, 157
Enivironmental level, 80, 83, 85
Enivironmental situation, 171
Enjambment, 117, 171
Episememe, 171
Ergativity, 171
Experience, three worlds, 1-2
Experiential component, 121
Experiential verbs, 171
Extended Standard Theory
  (EST), 59-60
Extension, 172
External rhyth, 115

Felicity conditions, 172
Fillmore, C.J., 50-57, 166, 169, 173, 178
Firth, J.R., 7, 77-78
Fodor, J.A., 19-20, 33-34, 37
Foot, 118, 172
Formal levels, 79, 145-148
Formal meaning, 85-87,
Formal translation, 152
Formation processes, 41
Formulae, elements of, 67, 68
Fowler, 119
Freeman, 117, 118, 139
Frege, G., 173
Fudge, 111, 133-134
Fuzzy sets theory, 36

Gardiner, A.H., 195
Gazdar, G., 195
Generative semantics, 30-34, 173
Genotype language, 64-65, 173
Given and New, 10, 129-130
Given information, 116
Givon, T., 74
Government theory, 63
Grammatical hierarchy, 147
Grammatical relations, 36-37
Graphational features, 83-84, 174

Graphematic units, 83
Graphological hierarchy, 144
Graphology meaning, 79
Grice, H.P., 37
Grosodic features, 83, 174
Gross, Maurice, 195

Halliday, M.A.K., 7, 10, 77-78,
    81, 86-88, 91-94, 106, 108,
    110, 131, 173, 179, 195-196
Halle, 117, 120, 134
Harman, G., 196
Hasan, 110
Hass, W., 195
Homonymy, 12, 174
Haspelmath, 110, 196
Hymes, 110, 111
Hyponymy, 174
Hypotatic relation, 174

Iambic heptameta, 134
Iambic pentameter, 134
Ideal figures, 104
Idea-label-idea relationship, 1-3
Ideational rhythan, 114,
Idiom, 175
Illocutions, 72, 175
Imagery, 112
Implications, 175
Implicature, 75-76, 175
Inchoative, 42, 176
Indeterminacy, 112, 176
Indices, 69
Inflectional units, 39-40, 48
Initial phrase-marker, 176
Institutional level, 80, 82
Intention, 10, 187, 189
Interactional component, 123
Internal rhythm, 115
Interpretation, 153
Intonational features, 83-85, 144
Intra-lingual interpretation, 153-154
Irony, 112

Jackendoff, R.S., 196
Jakobovits, L.A, 210
Jakobson, 98, 100

Katz, J., 19-23, 168, 173, 196
Keenan, 197
Kempson, R., 197
Key word, 110
Keyser, 117, 120, 134
Khaṇḍapakṣa, 3, 177
Kiparsky, P., 201
Knowledge, 38
Korg, 101
Krishnachaitanya, 100, 102
Krishnamurti, 100
Kunjunni, Raja K., 3-8, 14, 197
Kuntaka, 103
Kuppuswami Sastri, 100, 103, 105
Kuroda, 197

La Glay, M., 197
Label, 2
Lado, 159, 197
Lakoff, 25-30, 36-37, 197-198
Lakṣaṇā, 177
Langedeon, 196
Language,
    analysis
    levels of, 79-83
    functions of, 91-94, 172
    varieties, 82
Lasnik, 193
Lee, 104, 111, 198
Leech, 94, 198
Lehrer, 194
Levi, 199
Lexeme, 177
Lexical features, 148
Lexical item, 87-88, 177
Lexical units, 146-147
Lexis,
    formal levels, 147
    grammar and, 79, 145
Levion, 112, 113

Limpid style, 101
Linking coordination, 177
Literacy semounties, 100
Locutions, 72
Logical form, 61
Logical function, 92, 177
Longinus, 101, 104
Lutz, 117
Lyons, J., 167, 176, 198

Maclay, H., 57
Mammata, 104
Mukarovsky, 106
Markedness, 107-110, 177
Metre, 115, 178
Melody, 115
Meter rhythm, 115, 117
Marked themes, 130
Marked news, 130
Madhyama, 177
McCawley, J.D., 22, 25, 34
McIntosh, A., 195
Meaning
  apoha theory of, 6-7
  communication of, 2
  contextual approach to, 77-97
  factors, 12-14
  conveying methods of, 151-154
  features, 22-23
  language teacher and, 142-160
  learning ways of, 11-12
  meaning of, 1-3
  modes of, 142
  Modistae tradition of, 15-17
  Port Royal theory of, 17-18
  sphoṭa theory of, 4-5
Metaphor, 158, 178
Mīmāmsakās, 5, 10-11, 15
Modality, 51, 178
Modalization, 25
Modular theory, 63
Morgan, J.L., 75-76
Morphological component, 66
Motif, 81
Motive, 81

Naiyayikas, 5, 10-11, 15
Negation, 74, 178-179
Nesting construction, 24
New Information, 116
Newmeyer, 198
Nida, E.A., 150
Notion, the scale of, 90
Noun-verb relations, 43, 51-52

θ-theory, 63
Otoole, 98, 101
Ornate style, 107
Objective grammar, 179
Ogden, C.K., 199
Opacity, 72-73, 179
Operative-receptive distinction, 179, 183
Osgood, C.E., 199

Palmer, H.E., 165
Pandeya, R.C., 3, 6
Paradigmatic axis, 86-87
Paraphrase, 180
Parataxis, 180
Parenteau, P.M., 199
Parret Herman, 199
Participium, definition of, 16
Passives, 60-61
Patanjali, 4
Perceptual plausibility, 181
Performatives, 69, 181
Perlmutter, D., 36
Perlocutions, 72, 181
Phares, G.C., 199
Phonetic contiguity, 9
Phonegment, 84, 143, 181
Phonematic units, 83-84
Phonological meaning, 142-144
Poetic function, 100
Poetic effect, 100
Paradox, 102
Prominence, 103, 106, 110, 130-131
Proudhokti, 104
Pun, 112

Parallelisn, 113
Prese rhythm, 115
Phonemic clause, 119
Participant roles, 121
Polysemy, 181
Port Royal theory, 17-18
Postal, P.M, 36, 199
Potential content, 148
Pragmatic content, 94-96, 142-145, 148
Pragmatic presuppositions, 181
Pragmatic primes, 94
Pragmatics, 69-73, 181
Pragmeme, 94-95, 109, 182
Prakasam, V., 78, 84, 85, 119, 143
Predicate nominals, 30
Predication, 182
Preference semantics, 67-68
Presuppositions, 56, 69-71, 182
    feature, 23
Presupposition pool, 71
Process verbs, 42-47
Progressive differentiation, 182
Propositions, 51, 72-73, 182
Prosodic features, 83-84, 143-144
Psychological reality, 182-183

Ratnakirti, 6
Raqhavan, 101, 104, 105
Rasa theory, 99-102, 114
Riti, 100-101, 102
Rhythm, 106, 113-116, 184
Reinforced coupling, 113, 131
Redundancy, 183
    Revised Extended Standard
    Theory (REST), 59-60
Richards, I.A., 199
Rieux, J., 17-18, 200
Rivers, W., 158, 200
Rollin, B.E., 17-18, 200
Rommetveit, R., 200
Ross, J.R., 25, 36, 200

S-structures, 62
Saddock, J., 76, 200

Samnidhi, 184
Sandhi features, 143
Sankaran, A., 200
Sapir-Whorf hypothesis, 183
Scatter, 87, 191
Searle, J.R., 200
Selectional units, 39-40
Sellars, W., 194
Semantic ambiguity, 21
Semantic anomaly, 21
Semantic axioms, 65
Semantic component, 66
Semantic content, 94-95, 148
Semantic derivations, 65
Semantic features, 23
Semantic primes, 94-95
Semantic redundancy, 21-22
Semantic rules, 61-62
Semantic structure, 50-52
Semantic syntax, 26
Semantic theories, 21-50
    Shaumyan's, 65-67
Sememe, 94-95, 185
Semiotics, 69
Semi coupling, 113, 131
Stylistics, 98, 186
Sitapati, 119
Suggestion, 100
Syllable, 117
Svabhāvokti, 104
Silent ictus/stress, 120, 135
Sahrdaya, 105-106
Summative word, 110, 124, 186
Samatā, 113
Semantic rhythm, 114, 141
Stauffer, 116, 118
Stress maximum, 117, 134, 186
Stress neutralisation, 117
Setting selection theory, 20
Seuren, P., 25, 200
Sharma, D., 6, 200
Shaumyan, S., 64-67, 178, 201
Shuy, R., 191
Sign-ststems, 69

Simmons, J.S., 192
Sinclair, J. McH., 87, 201
Situation, 77-80
   feature, 89-90
Speech revelation, 8
Sphoṭa theory, 4-5
Staal, J.F., 201
Standard Theory (ST), 57-58, 164
State verbs, 42-46
Steinberg, D.D., 201
Substance, 79, 186
Suggestion theory, 5
Surpra features, 143
Surface structure, 39, 50-51, 55, 186
   deep structure and
   relations between, 58-59
Symbolozation processes, 41
Synonymy, 55, 121, 187
Syntagmatic axis, 86
Syntheticity, 187
System, 7, 187

Tarski, A., 201
Tate Allan, 99
Tillyard, E.M., 100
Tagore, 102
Thesis, 107
Tension, 115
Thesis rhythm, 115
Theme, 116, 187
   tomic stress, 116
Thomyson, 117
Tone group, 119
Textual component, 124
Tatparya, 9-10, 187
Templates, 67
Trace theory, 60
Transfer feature, 25

Transformation, 35, 61
Translation, 152-153

Uddeśya, 10, 188
Universal grammar theory, 62-63
Unity, 106, 110, 130-131, 188
Universe, 107, 110, 188

Vaisesikas, 11
Vakyasesa, 10
Valency, 199
Vakrokti, 102-104, 189
Verbal figures, 104
Verma, 108
Vāmana, 113
Verse line, 119
Value, 79, 85, 87
Vennemann, T., 26, 39, 71, 191
Verbs, 26, 39-40
   causative, 165
   Fillmore views about,
   semantic units of, 39-40
   types of, 44-47
Verma, S.K., 86, 201
Vidheya, 10

Walpole, H.R, 201
Weinreich, U., 23, 165, 201
Wilks, Y, 67-68, 201
Williams, Edwin, 201
Widdowson, 98
Wilde, oscar, 99
Welek, 101, 106
Warren, 101

Yogayata, 9

Ziff, P. 21

www.ingramcontent.com/pod-product-compliance
Lightning Source LLC
Chambersburg PA
CBHW071158160426
43196CB00011B/2119